W9-BDL-556

Thanks to our friends and others,
"who are friends we haven't met yet",
for your wonderful thoughts and
comments on Robert Isenberg's

Why Men Are Suspicious of Yoga
and Other Very, Very Funny Stories

Sharp mind + quick wit + just the right amount of 'bite' = a very funny set of short musings and stories. Do you feel like laughing? Do you need a humor fix? Don't miss this book. Thank you, Robert Isenberg, for your great storytelling talent!

Beth M

Really fun, easy reading- numerous antidotes to everyday situations. Easy to relate to as we have all done or experienced frustrating things. Eagerly looking for a sequel!

Steve W

WOW! Such a FUN diversion from all of the upsetting news around us! This book made me LAUGH with almost every page.

Fran D.

Robear's sharp wit and humor came through very clearly in these essays. This helps those of us who live in the rarefied suburbs to laugh at the absurdities of life. I particularly enjoyed the refrigerator who got a driver's license from the Registry. It's entirely believable.

K. Prager

As the old song goes, "Don't take it serious; it's too mysterious." Isenberg takes a witty and clear-eyed but gently wry look at his own life's adventures and foibles, which largely happen to be the same ones we all have. And if we don't laugh at ourselves and our situation, where is the joy?

CS

If you ever have a hard time falling asleep at night and want something funny and yet true to life, get this book.

Kai W

An uncanny observer of the human condition, Isenberg has a way of describing the mundane with both insight and humor.

Hal Miller-Jacobs

An entertaining read that made me chuckle and at the same time made me think. I loved the author's honesty and unapologetic view of his world, however politically incorrect it was. A good gift for your yoga teacher.

flowers

To understand Isenberg's writing style, mix equal parts Neil Simon with John Stewart, shake dry with an astute view of the world as it was, is and very well will be. From the nostalgic to the futuristic and everything in between, this book is a witty but tender romp. A must read!

Bella Rose Films

Take it on the plane...or read it at the commercials of your favorite show. It is a compilation of funny short stories that are relatable. There are too few things any more that make us laugh.

California

Robert has amazing storytelling skills. He can articulate what people are thinking with a very humorous spin. I found myself laughing aloud many times while reading these stories. A fun, easy read. Enjoy and let's hope he writes a few more books!

Reader

In the same vein as Phillip Roth, and John Irving with sprinklings of George Saunders.

tv yogi

Written with a sense of wonderment and a playful and unique outlook on everyday things. An ode to the ordinary.

Smiles and Chuckles

Like a box of gourmet chocolates --- eat one and you want to finish the whole box. Read one chapter and you want to read them all.

Suzi

"Why Men Are Suspicious of Yoga" by Robert Isenberg (aka "robear") is a series of autobiographical vignettes

that capture the humor in the little events of everyday life. Though the title suggests that the book may focus on the differences between men and women, the breadth of the book is much wider. In most chapters, Robear paints a picture. Like any good storyteller, he takes his time to set up his punchline; he sets the scene, presents the characters, and draws us into a story from his life. Easy, fun, and interesting read. Many are relatable to circumstances in one's life. A sure laugh for all.

Helene D.

It's unique! The book starts with several comedic scripts about syntax, morphs into multiple autobiographic episodes, and ends with a talking refrigerator. It makes a strong case that comedy and autobiography require an author who is pleased with who he is. The author is bright and well-travelled, who talks to himself when he would rather be talking to an audience. So why the good review? When you finish the book, you invest time and effort trying to figure out why you continue to think about it. If the book is a salesman, it made the sale.

Emily

SO funny and yet so real! Isenberg has crafted a classic, with a wide variety of different compelling stories. I LOL'ed my way from page 1 until the end.

Dave Kerpen

I breezed through the book in two sittings. I couldn't wait to read the next chapter to see what the author would come up with. Even some of the fantasies rang true.

Bill Morgenstein

Loved this book!! It's a funny but gentle commentary on real people and their struggles to make sense of an absurd world, which is sometimes of their own making!! Full of interesting and resonating ironies that linger with the reader. Perfect escape reading!! Looking forward to more!

A Happy Reader

My favorite bedtime snack is freshly stove-popped buttered popcorn. I'll eat handful after handful until I reach the bottom of the bowl and still want some more. Reading Robert's humorous essays was like that for me, and the price was right too!

Kim Ray Long

The book is at my bedside. I read a chapter a night, laugh, smile and go gently off to sleep.

M. Albin Morariu, M.D, Neurology

Many of the situations are just laugh-out-loud funny! I just finished and loved the book.
Funny and real situations to which most of us can relate. I hope there will be another book.

Dawn C. Ehrlich

Why Men Are Suspicious of Yoga

and Other Very, Very Funny Stories

Robert "robear" Isenberg

© 2018 All rights to text and images are reserved by Fairly Famous
Press and Robert Isenberg

ISBN 13: 9780692075753

Library of Congress Control Number: 2018902514
Robert Isenberg, Lexington, MA

Table of Contents

Dedication

To the Mighty Healing Power of Smiles and Laughter

A portion of the proceeds from the sale of this book will go to organizations that promote the healing benefits of laughter.

Mr. Fridge Rules

I just received the news. They want me to be a headliner in "robear's" book even though, unfortunately, the stories about me are in the back. Their newest idea is to place me at the beginning of each section. They will want me to wear different hats and caps.

I heard that so far they will have me in a baseball cap and a football helmet for the chapter called Games People Play.

For Language, I'll wear a scholar's cap.

For Family, a party hat.

For The World and Robert Meet, a French beret.

For Travel, a safari hat.

For Food, a chef's cap.

xvi   ROBERT "ROBEAR" ISENBERG

For Artificial Intelligence, can you believe there will be a full-size picture of me, Mr. Fridge, with antennas sticking out of my head?

They believe this will turn me into a huge celebrity. I'm not taking any bets on it. If it happens, I hope that I don't have to tour. I hate flying. Security is a big pain in my butt. When I go through security, they insist on opening all my doors. What really gets my goat is the stupid jokes they make about a refrigerator going through security. You'd think they'd never seen a refrigerator going through security before. One of the TSA guys said to his buddy as he scanned me, "We got a hot one here!"

Haw, Haw, they both thought it was so funny. I didn't!

If you think security is an issue, you should see me trying to get comfortable in those damn airplane seats. Impossible! Check out the person sitting next to me, especially when I place my arm down on the console so I can spread out the Wall Street Journal. I'll bet he can't wait to tell his wife that he sat next to a refrigerator who was reading the Wall Street Journal all the way to Baltimore.

Anyway, thank you, Mr. "robear", for writing this book and giving me an opportunity to be the coolest refrigerator on this planet!

Mr. A. Fridge

I

Language

1

Small Talk

I FOUND A two-page article in the Wall Street Journal about one word. The word is *"Maybe"*. Who would have thought the word *"Maybe"* would get to be such a big shot in the Wall Street Journal? *"Maybe"* recently came to prominence through Facebook. All of the many invitations I get on Facebook have the RSVPs asking for *"Yes","No"* and *"Maybe"*. According to the article, a *"Maybe"* can be anything you want it to be. It's really about the person interpreting the *"Maybe"*.

This made me think about the word *"Yet"*, which also rose to fame about fifteen years ago in a movie called "High Fidelity." The movie starred John Cusack. His girlfriend moves out and moves in with Cusack's upstairs neighbor. She comes back to Cusack's apartment to get the rest of her clothes. Cusack asks her, "Are you sleeping with our upstairs neighbor?" She answers, "Not *yet.*" This sends Cusack on a heart-wrenching search asking everybody he knows to define "*Yet*". Cusack wants to know, "Does this mean it hasn't happened "*Yet*", but it will happen? Or does it just mean very simply not "*Yet*"?

It's very much like "*Maybe*". It's all about the interpretation. After leaving the theatre, I began to think about the word "*Yet*". I realized that until I saw "High Fidelity", I had never given even five seconds thought to the word "*Yet*". Was I such a snob that a three-letter word like "*Yet*" was too small for me to consider?

This summer, my wife, Dana, and I were visiting some longtime friends and their nine-year-old daughter, Halley. They told a story that some of the school kids were teasing Halley by saying that her parents were old. Halley's response was "*So?*" Brilliant!!! She didn't need another word. "*So*" spoke volumes, so much so that I thought "*So*" should be in every politician's arsenal. I'm intending to write to President Obama and advise him that the next time he's attacked, he should just say, "*So?*"

"*So*" may look small, but it's definitely a bully! "*So*" set its sights on "*Very*". For many years, people would say, "Thank you '*VERY*' much." Now when accepting a gift or favor, just about everybody says, "Thank you '*SO*' much."

"*So*" is not only a bully; "*So*" is also an obnoxious braggart. "*So*" is always showing off by saying, "Look what I can do that "*Very*" can't do. "*So*" took a deep breath, exhaled and became "*Sooooo*". "*So*" can be as large or as little as "*So*" wants. It depends on the size of the favor or the size of the gift. "*Very*" is on the side lines watching and waiting. "*Very*" is practicing "*Very*" deep breathing.

Many other two-letter words can pack a mean punch. For instance, take the word *"That"*. Where would *"That"* be, without an *"Oh"* in front of it? It would be just *"That"*. But now *"That"* has some significance. It has some weight when someone says *"Oh That!"*

Same with the word *"Him"*. It has no special meaning until someone says ,*"Oh Him ."* It could be an impressive *"Oh Him"* or a dismissive *"oh him"*. It all depends on how one says the *"Oh"*. *"Issues"* are another one of those assertive bullies. We used to have *"Problems"*. The problem with *"Problems"* is that *"Problems"* are a dime a dozen. Nobody wanted to be bothered with somebody else's *"Problems"*. Almost everybody has their own problems. " *Issues"* are another matter. *"Issues"* have character. *"Issues"* command respect. People want to know what your *"Issues"* are. *"Issues"* have just about wiped away everybody's *"Problems"*.

"Oh" no, *"Maybe"* not. It's no *"Problem"*.

I'll just have to say *"So?"*

2

What Are Words Worth??

A WHILE AGO, I wrote a piece called "SMALL TALK." I suggested that the word *"So"* may look small, but it was definitely a bully. I also said that *"So"* is an obnoxious braggart. I explained what *"So"* had done to the word *very*.

For many years, when accepting a favor or a gift, most people would say, "Thank you very much." *"So"* being *"So"* set its sights on *"Very"*. Now people say, "Thank you *so* much."

When *"So"* applied for this job, it showed off by saying, "Look what I can do that *very* can't do!" *So* took a deep breath, exhaled and tiny *"So"* became *"Sooooo"*.

"So" grinned and offered, "I can be as large as you want me to be. It depends on the size of the favor or the gift you've received."

Now *"Very"* is still sitting on the sidelines practicing deep breathing.

I cannot tell you how many letters I received from both-fans of ""*Very*" and "*So*". Fans for "*So*" were upset that I had implied "*So*" had been underhanded in getting the job.

"*Very*" fans were just very upset.

One letter read, "I read your column about '*Very*' and '*So*'. I was FURIOUS! I've been using the phrase '*Thank you very much.*' all my life and I am not about to change now. This letter was signed "So what".

Another letter: "Dear Mr. Robear, don't you think there is enough competition in the world? You didn't have to pin '*Very*' against '*So*' to make your point." This letter was signed by Mr. I. Rate.

Someone just wrote, "*Soooooo* very troubled!!!"

It seems someone has dared to take on an even more inflammatory subject. I just discovered a book called, *Banish Boring Words* by Leilen Shelton. This book says the word "*Said*" is very boring.

I can only imagine the reaction of "*Said*" after it read this book. I'm sure "*Said*" would have said something like, "After all the times you people have used me, it finally comes to this? I guess you'll finally be happy when it's all been said." Never mind that they made a pretty successful movie called, *He Said, She Said*.

This writer doesn't stop with "*Said*". She wants the reader to be roused. For instance, she cites an example, "He backed away from the growling dog."

Her point is that this is a very boring sentence. Leilen's suggestion is, "Slowly and carefully, he backed away from the dog." My suggestion is that he ran like hell from the growling dog. Having had some experiences with growling dogs, the last thing I want to do is move slowly. When dogs growl, I don't worry about being boring.

This author even takes umbrage with the word *"Boring"*. In no uncertain terms, she argues that the word *"Boring"* is boring. How can the word *"Boring"*, which is so devastating, be boring? What is worse than being called boring? Trust me lady, in the world of name-calling, there are very few substitutes for the word *"Boring"*.

In the article about *"So"*, I also wrote about *"Yet"*. I mentioned that few people were able to define *"Yet"*. I'm truly grateful for the hundreds of letters I received, which defined *"Yet"*. Or should I say were trying to define *"Yet"*.

"Yet"'s biggest complaint is being misunderstood.

Someone wrote, "So, is the definition of *"Yet"* 'up until now', or 'at this time'?" They signed off with "I'll advise, but not yet."

3

What's Sooo Funny?

DAN, A WHITE-COLLAR guy, goes to prison. He's worried about fitting in, even more so as he looks around. That evening before bed check, his fellow prisoners are yelling out numbers. Whatever number is yelled out is received with bellows of laughter.

Dan asks his cellmate, Vladimir, "What's going on? What's so funny?"

Vladimir says, "Those numbers are all memorized jokes. We aren't allowed to tell jokes after dinner. We yell out the numbers we have given each joke."

"I really want to make some friends," says Dan. "Tell me what number is the funniest joke."

Vladimir says, "Try number eighty-six. That gets the biggest laughs."

Dan yells out, "Eighty-six!!!" Nothing!!

Dan turns to Vladimir and says, "What happened? You told me that the number eighty-six always gets huge laughs."

Vladimir looks at Dan and, with a straight face, says, "You just don't know how to tell a joke!"

I heard this story/joke many, many years ago. It's still true. Maybe truer than ever.

What Republicans find funny, Democrats usually don't and vice-versa.

For instance, Adlai Stevenson once said, "When the Republicans stop lying about us, we'll stop telling the truth about them!"

Most jokes and humorous stories depend a great deal on the audience. It also matters who is telling the story or joke. For instance, President Obama is probably considered witty by his supporters. His opposition would have said the joke only applies to him.

What does occur to me is that if a regular person were to use the president's material, it would do well to get a snicker.

Some months ago, we went to the Regent Theatre in Arlington to hear "Old Jews Telling Jokes." As it happened, I had heard almost every joke. Yet in most instances, I laughed. I guess professional actors make a difference.

One of their better jokes was a son asking his mother to come over to his apartment to meet three women he was dating. He wanted his mother to guess which one he was going to marry. After the women left, the mother guessed correctly!

"How did you know?" exclaimed the son.

"She's the one I hated the most!" frowned the mother.

I've noticed that telling jokes can be as competitive as Ping Pong. One man's joke usually leads to another man's joke. What is needed is a laugh meter.

Then there is the subject of comedians. Who is funny? Who is not! Some might find a comedian like Richard Pryor brilliant. I know I did. He was even able to make a heart attack funny. He did this by having his heart wrestle him to the ground, screaming, "I told you not to eat that bacon!!"

Another aspect of being funny is voice. Rodney Dangerfield had the perfect voice for, "My wife and I were happy for twenty years and then we met."

My wife, Dana, and I have been entertaining at senior residences for over seventeen years. I usually begin by telling the worst bad joke I know.

"What did one strawberry say to the other strawberry?" "If you weren't so fresh, we wouldn't be in this jam!"

It usually receives laughs and lots of groans. I tell this to see who is awake.

Sometimes I use one of my own lines to connect with an audience. "What is the sexiest thing one can say to their significant other? *You are right, dear!*" This usually receives knowing smiles and laughter.

I remember one of Woody Allen's classic stand-ups was that his wife was very immature. She was constantly trying to sink his tub toys. I was in a class in New York City with Woody Allen's first mother-in law. She insisted that Woody was not funny!! I wondered if she had been an accomplice in sinking Woody's rubber ducks.

Well!? Do you know how to tell a joke?

4

Forever and Ever

I MET HER at a Dairy Queen. The truth is, it wasn't really a Dairy Queen. It was a Dairy King, or maybe it was a Dairy Witch. Who cares? She was sitting at one of those outdoor tables. She was wearing navy shorts and a bright orange tank top. Her hair was jet black and her eyes sparkling blue. She looked up and smiled. She nodded hello and went back to her three scoops of dairy whip surrounded by banana slices, topped with strawberries and oodles of whipped cream.

I knew instantly she was in love with me. Hadn't she looked up from her banana split? It was obvious that she was enjoying her dish to the utmost. One only had to look at her face to sense her pleasure. Yet, she looked up at me. She was mine. I only had to say the right words.

I knew if this was a bar, I would most likely say, "Do you come here often?"

That would be a terrible start in a dairy bar. It might imply that she was overweight. No, no, it is best to come right out with it.

"I've been married twice. I would like you to be my third and forever and ever wife," I said.

She looked up from her banana split, "I'm concerned that I'd have to compete against your first two wives."

"Oh, I hadn't thought of that. But not to worry, if there were any sort of competition, I know you'd win easily."

"How can you possibly know that?" she asked.

"Easy! I'm the kind of guy who can take one look and just know things. I don't need to know any more about you than the way you were eating your banana split. In fact, I don't want to know any more about you."

"First of all, it's not a banana split. Here it's called "Bananas On Ice." Second, there are important questions to ask."

"Like what?" I wanted to know.

"Like my name. It's important in a wedding ceremony to know each other's names. You should also want to know if I'm married. Anyway, it's your lucky day. I just heard that my husband fell off a roof he was working on and was killed instantly."

"Very sorry," I said biting my lip, wondering what was coming next.

"Don't be sorry. You didn't know him."

"Are you okay?" I asked.

"Thanks, I'm drowning my sorrows in this 'Bananas on Ice'."

"How long were you married?"

"Who knows?" she said. "Maybe a year, maybe four years. I didn't count."

"Any kids?"

"No, thank you. He was always watching something stupid on TV. By the time he came to bed, I was asleep. Anyway, you said you didn't want to know anything about me and now here you go asking all these questions. How about you? What happened to your two wives? Did they fall off a roof?"

"The first marriage only lasted three months. I woke up one day and she said that this marriage had lasted way too long. She said she needed more space."

"What did you say?" she asked as she licked her spoon.

"No problem," I said. "When you come home from work, we'll talk about it."

She was a night watchman. She would probably be home before I left for work. I figured that she wanted a bigger apartment. Evidently, she left work early and left a note while I was sleeping. It said, *You were right. It's not a problem. I'm outta here. Please don't try to reach me!*

"What about your second marriage?" she asked, still licking her spoon. "Did she need more space too?"

"My second marriage lasted thirteen years, three months and a week."

"That's a long time—thirteen years. That's a long time to do anything," she said.

"She ran off with the local cobbler. I shouldn't say ran off. They live over on the next street from me. I could say *he nailed her.* I should have been more suspicious when she kept getting the same shoes resoled. Perhaps, I should have listened more closely when she spoke about the cobbler. She would quite often remark about his cute accent. She thought his joke about redoing the soles al dente was hysterically funny. Needless to say, I didn't."

"How long ago did she leave?" she asked.

"I dunno know. Maybe a week ago. Anyway, enough of the small talk. How does this weekend sound?"

"For what?" she asked.

"For getting married. You know, I swore I'd never marry again, but I hadn't seen you yet."

"You sure know how to romance a girl. What did you say your name is?"

"I didn't. It's Donald. Donald Gillis. Let's meet at the town hall on Saturday at twelve noon. You can give me your name there. Otherwise, I might forget it."

"I'll be there," she said. "Don't forget your birth certificate. Remember it's forever and ever."

5

Sticks and Stones

PERHAPS, WE *ELITISTS* have been wrong and the *Trump Deplorables* are right. Just perhaps he is onto something. After all, he demolished fifteen other candidates with his name–calling.

I hadn't thought of Jeb Bush as having "low energy" until, thankfully, Trump pointed it out. I was unaware of Marco Rubio's height until the now President started calling Rubio "Little Marco." Then there was "Lying Ted", i.e. Cruz.

One by one, they fell and not only did they fall, they actually seemed to take on the characteristic that Trump had stung them with. Jeb could barely respond to the barbs being hurled at him due to his low energy. Rubio seemed to shrink even more in stature. We always knew Ted Cruz was a liar; we were just too *sissy-liberal* to say it.

Trump wasn't quite as creative with Hillary. He called her "Lying Hillary," but with all due respect to Senator Cruz, he asked his permission, before he did it.

My question was how did the president learn to be so effective at name-calling?

I found out that he studied at over fifty-five playgrounds frequented mostly by eight-year-olds. The eight-year-olds were not chosen willy-nilly. First, the president and his teams studied a group of politicians and after a great deal of time and observation, they decided the polls were most likely to be affected by the slurs slung by eight-year-olds. He also noticed that the meaner the slur, the more tears that were shed. That was very important.

Wow! It turns out that President Trump's number one adversary is none other than North Korea's Kim Jong-un. Kim also prides himself on dishing out verbal abuse. It should be noted that not only are our military experts studying North Korea's nuclear arsenal but they are also studying Kim's over-the-top insults.

Both *leaders* have found their match. Kim Jong-un called President George W. Bush a "cowboy buffoon". He has also targeted his insults at most world leaders. Not to be out-done, President Trump has managed to insult most of our allies at one time or another.

It seems that these two great verbal swordsmen of our times are going face to face with insults. Kim Jong-un called Trump an "old lunatic!" Trump promptly retaliated with one of his wittiest retorts to date, calling Kim "short and fat."

Now I would have suggested that both could have done better, but it happens once again that I'm wrong! Kim was so hurt by being called "short and fat" that he has spent hours upon hours in front of a huge especially made mirror posing and stretching.

He has even sought out the very best psychiatrist in North Korea, who has assured him of the many wonderful features of being short. He told Kim, "You don't have to bend as much as tall folks." As for being fat, the psychiatrist explained that in North Korea, which is not known for good food, Kim has proven otherwise by his girth, which should definitely help his country as far as tourism goes. The psychiatrist makes sure to close their meetings by mentioning how handsome Kim Jong-un looks in his uniform.

President Trump has dealt with the "old" issue by putting on his favorite tank top and flexing his muscles one hundred times in front of Melania every evening before they go to sleep. The president also throws some jabs and mutters, "Kimsie, I'm going to make your nose even flatter!"

With some very good luck, these two characters will stick to insulting each other with similar witticisms and not take it any further!

6

This Is Not Fake News!

NEVER SPOIL A good story with the truth was always a treasured saying. Being able to spin a yarn, tell tall tales, have a touch of the blarney; these were all heralded qualities. Now, all of a sudden, people are demanding and expecting the truth. Anyone can deal with the truth. One just has to work a little harder when it comes to a fib.

Speaking of tall tales, President Trump has been insisting that he really won the popular vote and that hundreds of Massachusetts voters were bussed to New Hampshire in order to cast their ballots there to try to stop him.

I decided to investigate this situation and see if I could unravel the truth. It was far worse than I thought, or even President Trump imagined. After talking to well over one hundred persons, I discovered an underground organization called Operation Deplorable.

O.D.'s (as most of the insiders referred to it) goal was to bus Hillary's supporters to whichever states seemed to have the greatest basket of deplorable voters for Trump. That way, voters for Hillary could offset all those deplorable votes.

This discovery was just a tip of the iceberg. I found out that the reason the Tesla production had slowed was that Elon Musk had been commissioned to build humongous busses for O.D. These busses were fifty yards in length and had four levels. They could comfortably carry over nine hundred passengers and travel at astonishing speeds. It didn't stop there. Because of the brilliance of the Tesla organization, these busses could travel at over three hundred miles an hour undetected. They were manufactured to be invisible, not only to the human eye but to any state's radar. Tesla manufactured forty-three of these busses for O.D.

It was incumbent on O.D.s part to use the so-called Clinton machine to detect which states had the most Trump deplorables. Once this was detected, it was just a matter of rounding up the volunteers and packing them onto the busses.

One of the bonuses granted to these volunteers was that Hillary Clinton and Meryl Streep would send each person off with a pouch of homemade chocolate-chip cookies (no nuts).

Both Hillary and Meryl slaved over their respective ovens baking these cookies in time for the send-offs.

Another bonus was Cher Bono, who not only helped pass out these cookies but sang one of her most requested songs. Cher would hold up a portrait of Donald Trump and proceed to sing "It's in his kiss".

The volunteers could not have been more pleased. "Cookies and Cher!" they chortled. "I can't wait to tell my friends."

What could have gone wrong with this master plan? After digging in a bit more, I found the mistake.

Unfortunately for the Clintons, it was a big one. They had totally miscalculated the Midwest. They were all convinced that the Midwest harbored very few Trump deplorables and there was no need to send the busses there. Even James Carville was heard saying, "I've canvassed the Midwest many times. Those states are blue. We own them! Deplorables are not welcome there."

Hillary did win the popular vote quite easily because of O.D. but lost the electoral vote also because of O.D.

After finishing my self-designed project, I concluded that President Trump's suspicions were not wrong. He just didn't have the whole truth.

7

Read All About It!

C'MON! I CAN'T be the only one. They are everywhere—in supermarkets, in drug stores, service stations, convenience stores, everywhere. Somebody must be buying them, or they couldn't print them all every week. They certainly don't publish them for deadbeats like me.

What I do is almost as disgraceful as these tabloids. I look for long lines in the supermarkets. I particularly love it when somebody has a way overloaded cart in front of me. It gets even better if the person is fumbling for their money. This gives me a chance to nonchalantly pull one of these newspapers off the shelf and casually start thumbing through it.

Who was the genius that said, "Inquiring minds want to know?"

I can't be the only one who caught a glimpse of Hillary's photo with the headline, HILLARY CLINTON'S TWO SECRET STROKES. I guess they are not a secret anymore.

Am I the only one asking could this be true? Look at that photo of her!

The challenge now is to find the article. Unlike many magazines, the article's page is not listed anywhere. They know. They know that there are scum readers like me who want desperately to read these articles, but don't wish to buy the paper. It's not the money. It's the principal. It's bad enough that some stranger or checkout person would see me, a grown man, buying these magazines. But can you imagine if a neighbor spotted me with the paper? They would insist I was guilty of depreciating the entire neighborhood.

Somehow, it's different when another person in line sees you pull one down. They usually smile. You know that smile. It says, "Go ahead. I understand. I also want to know if Hillary had two secret strokes."

If it's a woman, that knowing smile is most likely saying, "It's HIM again! Who wouldn't have a stroke living with him? Look at that photo. She used to be attractive. Now look at her. That poor woman!"

I have the paper in my hand. I know I'm short on time. I check the line. There are still three people in front of me. Whew! I hope the cash register has one of those break-downs. Even better if one of these people in line can't find their credit card.

I start perusing for the article. On my way. Darn! "TV SHARKS FEUD EXPLODES"

I have to know. No, I tell myself, you really don't! You're still looking for Hillary.

I can sense the guy behind me is getting frustrated with me. He's pretending he's not looking over my shoulder. I'm surprised he hasn't pulled the paper out of my hands.

As I continue to turn the pages in hot pursuit of the Hillary article, I note that Queen Elizabeth was determined not to die before the birth of her grandson, who is William and Kate's new baby. This paper is predicting the child will be born with three heads.

I look up to check the line. I can feel the guy behind me breathing heavier. Too bad! He'll just have to wait till I find the article.

Finally, I find the Hillary article. There are more Hillary photos. They are not flattering. The article quotes Bill as saying, "Quit now!"

Now, I can believe a lot of things. In fact, I can believe a lot of things in this paper. But Bill giving up the opportunity of being First Man in the White House? Sorry, I cannot buy that.

Never mind being First Man. Just imagine how busy the presidency will keep Hillary.

"I'll have to be off on my own a lot. Wouldn't that be a shame?" old Bill would think.

Anyway, the article explains the secret strokes.

I think to myself, "Why do I waste my time reading the *N.Y. Times*? Even worse, the *Wall Street Journal*? There is really no comparison if you wish to stay awake."

8

A House Divided

SOME SAY THE country has never been more divided. Some point to Donald Trump and Hillary Clinton as divisive candidates. I'm not so sure that the situation is any different than it always has been. One just has to look under the covers.

A recent article in a newspaper was entitled "Why Facts Don't Unify Us." It stated that *once people have made up their mind on whatever theory, the last thing they want is to be bothered by the facts. Some of our preferences are based on various ideologies. However, recent research shows that even scientific proof means absolutely nothing in changing minds.*

A few years ago, I read an article in the Wall Street Journal that mentioned that Dunkin Donuts offered $200 to Starbucks patrons to try Dunkin Donuts and vice versa. The Starbucks clientele generally responded by saying *Puh-lease*. Dunkin Donuts loyalists were more outspoken. Some of them commented on the Starbucks layout, *If I wanted to sit on a couch, I'd have stayed home!* Others rebelled at the Starbuckian language. Many commented that they didn't know what *Vente* meant and they didn't want to know either. Talk about divides!

I recently noted that there is a club that has been meeting for over forty years to celebrate Mr. Peanut. These people call themselves Nuts. They actually have annual conventions where they meet once a year to collect and trade memorabilia.

They consider Mr. Peanut a dapper dude. He will strut around in different costumes depending on the weather and the location. He is never seen without his cane. It has been said that at one of these memorabilia parties, a Mr. Peanut cane will sell for over a thousand dollars. It's difficult to find fault with the name Nuts.

Not to be outdone, a raspberry jam club formed about ten years ago. The Nuts have no use for the Jammers, as the jam club refers to their membership. The Nuts say the Jammers are just a seedy bunch. The Jammers also insist it should be jam & peanut butter sandwiches, not peanut butter and jam. Their goal is to come up with a character to take on Mr. Peanut and they are sticking to it.

If we think that there is a bitter rivalry between Boston & NYC over the Red Sox and Yankees, then listen up regarding LeClair, Iowa, and Fort Byron, Illinois. These two cities have a tug of war every year worth $8,000 to the winning city. The WSJ makes light of this rivalry with such corny comments as "*Losing to Illinois at Tug of War puts Iowa at the end of its rope.*" They also go on as to what a *stretch* all this excitement is. This all started as a friendly rivalry. It's anything but that now. Hateful bumper stickers have evolved. Rumors of cheating have emerged. In the case of the Red Sox, it's basically a case of rooting for strangers. This tug is personal.

This divisive madness first came to my attention many years ago. We joined a swim club that had an extremely large pool. At the time, our two daughters were quite young and just learning to swim. As a result, we only went to the shallow end of the pool to accommodate our kids. On one beautiful afternoon, my children were away. I decided to try the other side of the pool. I pulled up a chair and overheard a conversation by two people who had seemingly just met.

It started with, "Nice day, isn't it?"

The second person responded, "Yes, it certainly is."

First speaker, "It's so lovely over here."

Second speaker, "The trees are higher on this side. The shade is so delightful."

"Yes, and do you notice that even the people on this side are much nicer."

9

Where Has All the Humor Gone?

THERE WAS A time when there was some humor in politics. There was a time when comedians were very funny about politics.

Will Rogers made a handsome living telling political jokes. Some of them even resonate today.

For example, he once stated, "Alexander Hamilton started the U.S. Treasury with nothing. It was the closest our country ever came to being even."

He also noted, "I'm not a member of any organized political party. I'm a Democrat!"

And he is said to have reported, "I don't make up jokes. I just watch the government and report the facts."

Stephen Colbert watches President Trump and reports what he says. Is it funny?

I guess if dark humor is funny, then perhaps, it's funny. Colbert shows Trump mentioning that there were "fine" people on both sides in Charlottesville. One side boasted neo-Nazis, KKK alumni, and White Supremacists. This group was carrying torches, flags with swastikas and crying out racist remarks.

What's funny here? Is it funny that our president can actually say that "fine" people are in such a group? Then elaborate by adding, "And you know that too!!" I wonder if even Will Rogers could find humor here.

There was a time when politicians dropped lines that some of us thought were funny. For instance, President Johnson complained, "If I walked on water in the morning, in the afternoon, the press would comment that it was because I couldn't swim."

President Kennedy was a master at self-effacing humor. His wit sparkled with such gems as these: "My dad called me and shouted, 'Don't buy one more vote than necessary. I'll be damned if I'm going to pay for a landslide!' I took him at his word."

Regarding appointing his brother, Robert, to be the attorney general of the United States, President Kennedy quipped, "I don't see anything wrong with giving Bobby a little legal experience before he goes out on his own to practice law."

The concept of humor was a huge factor in Kennedy's quest for the presidency, so much so that he actually hired Mort Sahl. Sahl was one of the younger comedians of that time. I remember that Sahl was credited with saying that President Eisenhower had kept us out of Mars.

William F. Buckley, when he ran for mayor in NYC, snorted, "If elected I'll demand a recount!"

Bob Hope, much like Will Rogers, used political material very successfully. One of my favorite lines is, "I didn't realize how poor our economy was until I received a Care Package from an Ethiopian." At the time, and still now, Ethiopia's economy was in desperate straits.

In deference to President Trump, he did utter one line during the campaign that caused me to smile. He said he didn't understand why Michelle Obama got so much credit for her speech and his wife, Melania, got dissed for giving the same exact speech.

Trouble is, I'm not sure he was joking.

The entire presidential race was mostly humorless. The theme was insults and barbs. For the most part, Hillary was devoid of any humor. Her only attempts were to comment that this was the first time she ran against anybody whose hair was more controversial than hers. She also grieved that Trump would probably rate the Statue of Liberty only a three.

So I Say, *WHERE HAS ALL THE HUMOR GONE? LONG TIME PASSING. LONG TIME AGO.*

II

Games People Play

10

Harvey's Mother's Funeral and the Sunday Morning Tennis Game

IT WAS LATE Friday afternoon at the office. The phone rang. I picked it up. It was Harvey.

"What do you want?" I shouted. "Can't you see I'm very busy?"

"My mother's funeral is on Sunday at 9:00 A.M at Stanetsky's Chapel in Vinnin Square," Harvey said.

"I didn't know your mother died." "She didn't," Harvey said.

"So how can you have a funeral for your mother if she's not dead?" I asked.

"What do you think? It's a restaurant? You can just call ahead and tell them to hold a casket? This takes planning. You need a firm reservation. This is Stantesky's! There is a long line of people dying with reservations at Stanetsky's.

Anyway, my mother is dying. My brother, Billy, is flying in from Vegas."

"Wait a second!" I said. "Just because Billy is flying in from Vegas does not mean your Mom has to die and keep the appointment at Stanetsky's?"

"She's having trouble breathing," Harvey said. "I don't think she'll make it through the night."

"Wait another second. Your mother! She's only ninety-eight years old. Since when will a little trouble breathing stop her from living? Your mom went toe to toe with Henry Kissinger at the Massachusetts General when she was recovering from her heart attack. Remember your mother telling us how she understood every word that Professor Kissinger said. Your mother also said that the professor agreed with all her opinions. Besides, what if she doesn't die? Do you have a substitute to fill in for your mother at Stanetsky's?" I asked. "And by the way, have you called Sal yet?"

"No, I haven't had a chance. Will you do it for me?" Harvey asked.

Sal has arranged all of our Sunday morning tennis games for the past twenty-five years - the place, the time, the players. Sal takes this task very seriously. Sal has been known to consider fining someone who calls in late on a Friday to report an illness and an inability to play on Sunday.

As soon as Harvey hung up, I called Sal. "Harvey has arranged for his mother's funeral on Sunday morning," I said.

"I didn't know his mother died," said Sal.

"She hasn't," I said.

"So how can there be a funeral if Harvey's mother hasn't died?"

"I know. I asked the same question."

"Well, if she hasn't died yet," Sal said, "couldn't they arrange the funeral for another day?"

"No," I said. "Seems to be set in stone."

"What time did you say the funeral will be?"

"Nine A.M," I said.

"But that's the time we play tennis. Can't they make it later in the day?" asked Sal.

"No," I said. "It's set for 9:00 A.M. No changes. Whether his mother shows up or not."

"I'll have to think about this," Sal said and hung up the phone.

I called Harvey back and said, "I called Sal."

Harvey said, "What did he say?"

"He wasn't happy," I said. "In fact, he was quite upset."

"About my mother?" Harvey asked.

"No," I said, "About the tennis game."

"Are any of the guys coming to the funeral?"

"I asked Sal that question. Sal didn't think so. He said they told him they had a hard enough time getting up early on Sunday for tennis. He didn't think they could get up for a funeral. He also said he cancelled the court. There wasn't enough time to get any substitutes."

In the meantime, Sal had already arranged for the next Sunday's game. He seemed to be pulling himself together after the shock of having to cancel our Sunday morning tennis game for the first time in twenty-five years.

Harvey's mom made it through the night. She died at six thirty-eight A.M. on Saturday morning.

The funeral took place at Stanetsky's on Sunday at nine A.M. The eulogies were quite beautiful and fitting. Harvey's mother, Mildred, was a saint.

11

How Do We Know We Care?

GETTING READY TO leave the office, I moved quickly as I didn't want to be late for the tennis game. I had covered my body with multiple braces. I picked up a plastic cup and swallowed two Tylenols. There was always some water left in the cup. I threw this on the three plants that lived in the hallway outside the office door. The plants had aged. They had been sitting there for more than twenty years. However, they were alive, though somewhat withered.

I didn't want to be late. I could hear the wise cracks in my head.

"Oh, look who showed up."

"Nice of you to come."

The tennis game with this group, like the plants in the office hallway, had gone on for over twenty years. Now the game was more about clever remarks and quick verbal responses rather than tennis shots.

The guys were impatiently waiting as I arrived.

Alfie looked at his watch and yelled, "Do you need a crutch?"

Tommy laughed, "Hey, let's get started before we fall asleep."

Jim smiled, "I'm impressed that you guys are still standing. I figured out the sides. Alfie and I against you two."

"You mean I've got Tommy!" I said sounding sad. "Only kidding."

For the next hour and a half, there could be heard:

"For heaven's sake!"

"There he goes cursing again."

"Do I look like I would make a bad call?"

"I quit!"

"We should be so lucky."

The chatter continued. "I noticed a tennis court at a senior residence. I should have made a reservation for us there."

"I'm surprised when you perform at those places that they don't lock the doors on you," laughed Alfie.

I had to get back to the office. I needed to finish some work. As I drove back, I was thinking that our most valuable player now is the one who can hear the score and still remember it five minutes later.

The office hallway was very dark. Pushing the hallway door open, I tripped on something. I fumbled for the light so I could see what I had tripped over.

"My G-d, the plants are gone! Who would take the plants?"

The outside doors were locked. It had to be an inside job.

They weren't exactly valuable objects. Maybe I'll call the police. I'll tell them my plants are missing. Right. I can just hear the cops.

"Plants?! Hmm. Would you repeat that, Sir? Could you describe these plants? About how tall would you say they are? You say they were a brownish, green color? Would you like us to send out an all-points bulletin on these plants?"

I decided it was probably not a good idea to call the police. I went home.

"Did you guys play tennis tonight?" asked my wife, Dana. "My friends are always asking if those aging guys are *still* playing?"

"Speaking of aging, you know the hall plants in the office? They're gone!"

"The what did you say were gone? The plants? Are you sure?"

"Of course, I'm sure! Do I look like the sort of person who would say something is gone if it's not?"

"How could they be gone?" asked Dana. "What do you think? They got tired of just sitting in the hallway and left?"

"Very funny. I watered them at 6:15, came back at 9:15 and they were gone. They didn't even leave a note."

"Did you call the police?" asked Dana.

"No, I didn't."

"Tomorrow, we'll go on a plant hunt. We'll find them dead or alive," smiled Dana.

The next day, I asked Karen, my secretary, if she noticed anything different as she came in the office.

"Nooo. Why?"

"Didn't you notice? The plants are gone."

"What plants?" Karen appeared puzzled.

"*What plants?* The plants that have been in the hall for twenty years," I exclaimed.

"Are you sure?"

"Of course, I'm sure! Do I look like the kind of person who would say something is gone when it's not?"

Karen rarely got out of her chair. She got up. She went into the hall, came back and said, "You're right. Did you call the police?"

"No, I didn't. Thanks for conceding that I'm right."

"Anyway, those plants were getting old," said Karen.

"Speaking of old, did you and your buddies play tennis last night?"

"Thanks a lot," I growled.

Weeks went by with no sign of the plants. At the end of most days, I found myself filling the watering can with no place to pour it.

Two months later, as I fumbled for my keys and opened the office door, there were the plants! They were back! A tiny piece of paper was tucked under the plant holders.

Thanks for the use of your plants. My daughter got married. We used the plants at the ceremony. It meant a great deal to all of us that the plants were not young, but still going strong. Thank you so very much for caring for them so diligently. Sincerely, Your Anonymous Neighbor.

12
Fanned Out!

IT WAS QUITE a few summers ago on a Friday night. It wasn't that late. Nearing eleven P.M., The Red Sox were playing Seattle, a mediocre team. The Red Sox were ahead three to nothing. Seattle was up with two outs. It was the top of the ninth with nobody on base. Koji was pitching for the Red Sox.

Koji had been one of the main reasons the Red Sox won the pennant and World Series last year. He was also having another good year despite the fact that at the time, the Red Sox were trailing the league-leading Orioles by fifteen games. I would be going up to my bedroom in a few minutes content that the Red Sox won the opening game of what would be a three-game series. Forty minutes later, Seattle was celebrating a five to three victory. I turned off the TV.

I wasn't sure exactly how it all happened. If it could go wrong, it did go wrong. Squeaky pop-ups fell in. *A baseball nightmare coming true.* What was worse was that I couldn't fall asleep. Here I was lying in bed feeling horrible that the Red Sox lost another game. "Why?" I asked myself. "It makes no sense. None! Why should I care? My life will not change one iota whether the Red Sox win or lose. None of them come from around here. And even if they did, so what! Did any Red Sox player ever come around to my office and ask if I were having a good week?" I lie there in bed asking myself which is worse, feeling terrible that a bunch of strangers lost another ball game, or that I felt terrible about feeling terrible that a bunch of strangers lost another ball game?

I always decline whenever I'm asked to go to the ball game at Fenway Park. Who wants to sit in that traffic? Who wants to sit on those uncomfortable seats? Who wants to smell the aroma of beer? Not me!

Of course, plenty of others do. The Red Sox are one of the teams with the best attendance in baseball, if not the team with the very best. I see the fans sitting there on my television, praying for the Red Sox, praying for a bunch of MILLIONAIRES to win a game of baseball"

And yes, for a moment, I feel superior to those people who put up with all the aforementioned discomforts while I sit in my family room on a recliner watching my wide screen TV.

But, and this is a very big BUT: those who choose to buck the traffic, to sit on those awful seats, and smell the beer don't have to put up with the TV ads.

In between innings or when a new pitcher is coming in, a fellow with a pony tail tells me why I should come to his store to buy a mattress. His store is called the official furniture store for the Boston Red Sox. I have no idea what or why that should mean anything to me.

The food ads don't stop. I know that they're not only bad for my stomach, the ads are bad for my head. A coffee company is telling me the Red Sox run on their coffee. A very poor slogan this year.

The insidious, most often repeated ad rant is *"When the moment is right."* They generally show a couple staring into each other's eyes and smiling, that one and only smile. And there I am alone in my recliner, wondering why no matter which couple they picture, they all end up in a bathtub. Why a bathtub? Did the guy say something stupid? In any case, the Red Sox who are also taking a bath are not taking any ownership of that company.

It's a tradeoff: *traffic on Yawkey Way or ads?*

I'm back in my bed twisting and turning. Dana who had been reading looked over to me, "You didn't have to watch. I could have told you the result."

I'm still feeling bad that I feel bad. I lie there swearing to myself that it's over. We have finally split. I mean the Sox and I. I will not watch another game...until...until tomorrow night.

13

How Sixty Minutes Became Three and a Half Hours

IT WAS A Thursday evening. I could not think of anything better to do, so I decided to watch Thursday Night Football. I thought it would be an interesting game: the Detroit Lions against the Green Bay Packers. Both teams had been erratic during the year. Green Bay had been heavily favored in their first meeting, so, of course, Detroit had won.

Sounds interesting. However, I never realized I could learn so much about mattresses.

It seems that every few minutes, and I mean a few, a different salesperson would come on the screen to explain why I needed his or her mattress NOW! I actually went upstairs to check on what was wrong with my own mattress.

When the mattress commercials were not being displayed, there was Bobby Dylan advertising IBM. Bob Dylan, the all-time hipster! A dude before there were dudes. The all-time anti-establishment character! Yes, it was a very old and wrinkled Bob Dylan hustling for IBM. Would Boston's Mayor, Walsh, come on next and tell me why I should be rooting for the Yankees and the Jets?

"FOOTBALL IS FAMILY!" said the next commercial.

Really?? Not any family I know.

The screen flashed back for a few seconds and someone punted a football.

Then in a flash, Duluth underpants were having a brawl with a grizzly bear. It turned out to be no contest. Duluth won pretty easily. I thought maybe Duluth won because I was rooting for the bear. A few minutes later, Fruit of the Loom came on explaining why their underwear was better. It definitely was more colorful. I have to confess. Once again, I went upstairs to look in my underwear drawer. I was very disappointed with what I saw.

Then the car ads began to whiz by me. Every once in a while, I would get to see one of the quarterbacks completing a pass. From time to time, a score would flash up. Detroit was ahead 17 to 0.

BMW was advertising that their brake service was only $239. Wait a second! I had not even considered buying a BMW, yet they were insisting on selling me a brake job.

GMC had people musing in disbelief that the car they're sitting in is a GMC. We are also told they are real people. I'm guessing as opposed to non-real people.

Someone recovered a fumble for a touchdown. The score is now 20 to 14. How did all this happen? Where was I?

Worse were the food ads. I could not believe how good Wendy's 4 for 4 Bacon Cheddar Burger looked. I was salivating! Then there were two young men munching and loving their burgers. Out of nowhere, a cow appeared. This cow looked sadder than any cow ever, and that's not easy. She looked at the young men with tears in her eyes. A sign for Chick-fil-A appeared. It read, "Why not eat more chicken?" There were medical ads for a whole bunch of stuff I never heard of, all having more side effects than their cures. The side effect I found most bothersome was from using Cialis. All the users seemed to end up in bathtubs. No thanks! I prefer showers!

The game is over. Detroit won 23 to 21 NO?? NO!!!! Detroit committed a foul! Green Bay got one more down. A Hail Mary! Green Bay 27, Detroit 23! And I was rooting for Detroit!!

Oh well, there's always my mattress.

III

Family

14

Brothers

I CAME INTO Room 1024 at Mass General. My brother, David, looked up and, between his teeth, muttered, "Rat Bastard Squealer Brat."

I was stunned, not only because he could barely speak due to the tubes coming out of all sides of him but he still managed to find the strength to call me *Rat Bastard Squealer Brat.*

David is older than I. He never found my existence to be comfortable, or for that matter, acceptable. I, on the other hand, idolized him. As a pre-teen, I couldn't do enough for him. I lied for him. I took the food off my plate for him. All in all, I groveled for him.

As I grew into my teens, the situation got worse. David got his driver's license and soon after, a rat-trap car. I still had a bicycle.

One especially hot day at our house in Dorchester, I was mowing the lawn. He pulled up in his car and called out to me, "I'm going to the beach. Do you want to come?"

"Sure," I said and ran to his car.

"Just checking," he said as he sped off down the road, leaving me standing there.

Of course, I reported his evil deed to our mother.

A few years later, I had a night job and arrived home around midnight on a regular basis. Although there were many empty rooms in my parents' house - our older siblings had left years before - neither David nor I would give up ownership of the room that we shared.

I considered it important to make sure my late arrivals were known to the sleeping David. I would ask him if he were awake. After he growled his answer, I would say, "Just checking." This was usually around one or two in the morning. David had a job that required him to rise at about six.

One morning, for "getting even reasons" known only to those who have siblings, he put the alarm radio to my ear and raced out of the bedroom. I awakened with a start when the thing went off and chased him into the kitchen. He stood with his back to the refrigerator repeating, "Come on buddy boy! Come on buddy boy!" His hands were behind his back. I flew at him. He quickly jerked his hands out from behind his back and revealed a full pitcher of orange juice, which he proceeded to throw all over me. Now orange juice in the morning can be refreshing. This wasn't! Have you ever spilled orange juice on the floor? It's pretty sticky, right? Imagine a whole pitcher of defrosted "Minute Maid" dripping from my hair to my toes.

My mother, hearing the yelping, came rushing down the stairs. She was screaming, "What's wrong with you two! You'll kill each other. You'll be the death of me. Maybe then you'll be happy!!"

"He started it," I assured my mother.

I remember our last big fight. It was on his wedding day. David was to marry Amy Silver that afternoon. I was to be his best man and, as his best man, I believed it was my duty to tell him he was making a grievous mistake to marry Amy. For some reason, this upset him. It had poured the previous evening. This didn't stop us from punching, wrestling and rolling around on the still very wet and muddy ground in our tuxedoes.

I had my reasons for trying to break up the wedding. I had very good reasons! About three months before the wedding day, the three of us had driven to New York City. Our first stop was to be the Carnegie Deli. David and his fiancé, Amy, would live park while I ran in and picked up two extra-large hot pastrami sandwiches. Amy swore she was dieting and didn't want any, though I offered to split my sandwich with her. She said she had brought along a salad for herself and that would be more than enough.

When I got back to the car, I handed Amy David's sandwich, which she quickly unwrapped and took a humongous bite before giving it to David. I had entrusted her with a Carnegie Deli hot pastrami sandwich and look at what she did! How could you trust such a woman, never mind talk of marrying her?

Now, my mother came running out of the house and tripped. "Look what you two good-for-nothings made me do. See, you'll be the death of me yet. Then you'll be happy!!"

"He hit me first," I said to my mother.

"And on your brother's wedding day when you are supposed to be his best man. The both of you should be ashamed!" our mother shouted. "Look at what you have done to your clothes. In front of the house yet, for everybody to see!"

Let's skip forward some twenty-five years. David, divorced and now my good friend, was dating this one and that one.

And then I met Dawn at my wife's high school reunion. She was laughing with another woman. I was interested in her, so I introduced myself and asked where her husband was. She told me that she would be signing her divorce papers in a week.

"Are you dating?" I asked.

"No, not planning on doing that for a while," she said. "Why do you ask? Are you asking me out?"

"No, not me. I'd like you to meet my brother."

I saw her checking me out. Then, she asked, "Is he much like you?"

I wasn't sure how to respond. I took a shot and lied. "Yes," I said.

"Okay," she said.

I had some work to do to get David to agree to meet her! The problem: she was about 5' 10". He was not.

His first question was, "How tall is she?"

"About the same height as us," I lied again.

They have been "going together" now for about twenty-four years. In fact, they live together. He is still very miffed though that I lied about her height.

Visiting David in Room 1024 at Mass General Hospital, I asked, "Why are you calling me a Rat Bastard Squealer Brat?"

"Because you squealed. You were always a lousy squealer," he said.

I knew what he was talking about. You see, I had spoken to David on Thursday and to me, he sounded really sick. When I asked if he had a doctor's appointment, he said, "Next Monday."

I said, "Next Monday is four days away. You should see a doctor immediately."

"Mind your own damn business," David replied.

In response, I called his doctor's office and spoke with the secretary. I told her that my brother was very sick and needed to see the doctor immediately. "Impossible. He is fully booked and besides, your brother has an appointment on Monday," she said.

"Please speak to the doctor. My brother is very sick and must see the doctor today," I pleaded. "Please, please ask the doctor if he could just squeeze David in! It's an emergency!"

She said she would call me back and she did. "The doctor will see David at 4:00 P.M. today," she said.

Now I had to get David to the doctor without letting David know what I had done. I called Dawn on her cell phone and asked her to tell David that she had received a call from the doctor's office and that he would be unable to see David on Monday. He needed David to come in at 4:00 P.M. today instead. David saw the doctor at 4:00 P.M. and ended up being rushed to the hospital. I thought I was safe, except Dawn squealed on me!

When I went to visit David, Dawn met me in the hospital lobby and confessed that she had told David the whole truth.

"Rat Bastard Squealer Brat," David growled almost inaudibly when I entered Room 1024 at the Mass General Hospital. David's glazing glare turned towards Dawn.

Dawn looked at me and smirked, "Bobby started it."

15

The Practice Run

WHEN I WAS fourteen, I had this thing about almost all of my friends' mothers. "This thing" was that I wanted to make love to them. For the most part, they were in their late 30's or early 40's. To me, they were all extremely mysterious and fascinatingly attractive. I thought about them all the time!

From my perspective, their husbands were all preoccupied with their work. When they weren't at work, they were probably washing their cars. They were overweight, bald or balding; in short, little competition. Here I was, all of 14, a literal ball of fire. Sure, I was without experience, but that would be a plus since these women would be my coaches. Best of all, I could learn from them just how to please them, which I would be more than willing to do. Of course, I knew that they had *done it*. Weren't my friends, their sons, living proof?

My plans were to visit one of them when I knew my friend was out and tell his mother I would wait 'til he came home. Once in the house, I thought I was half way home. Of course, connecting or having a stimulating conversation could be a bit of a hurdle. Where were their interests? What were they thinking about? Mine were somewhat limited. Usually, how many guys would show up for the after-school ball game and what was for supper?

How was I going to reach out to these women? Perhaps, I should get right to the point. Once in the house, confess my fantasy. Tell them that I had become obsessed with their beauty and grace. It was the truth! Their every movement brought flutters to my pelvis.

I decided I needed a practice run. My oldest brother was married with kids. He lived in a two-family house. His family occupied the bottom floor and his widowed sister in-law lived upstairs. She was about thirty, a little young for my taste, not the same wonderful age as my friends' mothers, but she had a vacancy. She had lost her husband. Surely, she would recognize this young stud and put his potential talents to use.

So I told my brother, "Any time you need someone to babysit, I'm available."

I soon noticed that she had many male friends, but they too struck me as stodgy, unappealing and really a physical joke next to my youth. I got very clever about when to listen for the goodbyes, the deep-throated parting kisses on the stairs, the sighs and the grunts. Somehow I knew she knew I was listening!

One night after one of those losers tripped his way out, she knocked on the door. I rushed to the door. There she was wearing a tank top and short shorts. She had an unlit cigarette between her sexy lips.

Oh my God, this was it. She would no doubt see the growth in my pants. She would see it and unquestionably have to have it. I was shaking.

"Did your big brother leave any matches around?"

I thought, "Oh my god, matches! Red hot. "Matches!" She is really coming on to me. Have I got a match for you!"

She smiled knowingly, looked me up and down and said, "Right now, I want a match for my cigarette. So find me one quickly. Right now, I want a cigarette before I go to bed."

"Bed?" Oh my God, she said "bed." How blatant could she be?

I knew that when she said "right now," there was more coming after the "right now."

I also knew the match request was a poor excuse for what she really wanted. I was certain that after the cigarette, she and I would bed down.

I ran into the kitchen. I found some matches. I flew back to her. She took them, grunted a thanks, turned, opened the door and slammed it behind her.

"Goodnight," I whispered, with a sigh of relief. I caught a break. I could now finish my homework.

16

Butchy A.K.A. Sonny

BUTCHY WAS DISGUSTING! Butchy lived across the street from me. He was not my favorite neighbor. He was very grubby, overweight and usually very smelly. I thought Butchy was living proof that man had descended from apes. I saw him almost every day. Usually, it was his feet that I saw, sticking out from under a car that he and my brother were meddling with. We seldom spoke. Our entire communication was the sneer Butchy cast on me.

Growing up, he was always Butchy. Years later, he opened a gas station that also repaired cars. He called it Sonny's. Why? I was never sure. He had a brother whom everyone called Sonny. Perhaps, it was because of his brother. Anyway, soon after, he opened the station. Everyone began calling him Sonny. I'm sure he liked being called Sonny better than Butchy. The garage was perfect. Now he could be as grubby, smelly and sloppy as he wanted and be admired for it. The dirtier, the better! When customers brought their car in and told Sonny their problems, they certainly felt they were talking not only to the owner but to the guy, the man, *an automobile genius.* Sonny would open their car hood and after a few curses and tsk-tsks, he would mumble how long it would take for repair—if he could get the parts. Comfort set in. After all, they were talking to Sonny. Who cared if he smelled? Who cared that he had a grease stain stretching from his hairy, hairy forearm to the top of his shirt and on to his left cheek? I envied his insolent confidence and his perpetual sneer at my automotive incompetence.

I had purchased my first automobile. I was the fifth owner of a very temperamental M.G.A. It would never start in the winter and it overheated in the summer. I spent a lot of time at Sonny's. Sonny called my M.G.A. a "sewing machine with wheels." He seemed to save his snottiest sneers for my M.G.A., especially when it was helplessly towed into his garage.

Spending so much time at Sonny's, I began to notice his clientele. I noted that quite a few of them were women, including Mrs. Seid. Mrs. Seid lived next door to me. She and her daughter, Rachel, had been a very meaningful part of my fantasy life. I found them both exquisite. I used to refer to them as flawless. Unfortunately, for me, my mother had a huge argument with Mrs. Seid. I was not allowed to speak to any of the Seids. I suffered from long distance lust. Sonny always seemed to be much nicer to the women who came in, especially to Mrs. Seid.

The years passed. Sonny, having made quite a bit of money, retired to Florida. My brother, David's friendship with

Sonny seemed to have flourished over the years, even with the distance, or perhaps because of the distance.

David decided to throw a party for both his old and new acquaintances. As I entered David's house, I saw him. He was standing in a far corner with a drink in his hand. He was alone. It was Butchy, or maybe he was still Sonny in Florida. I didn't know or care.

It was time for me to put aside my petty resentments. It was time for me to grow up. It was time for me to go over and talk to "whatever his name was" man to man.

I accepted the challenge. In seconds, we were facing each other. I had no idea what to say, so I said, "How are you?"

He grunted a minimal inaudible reply.

I continued, "How do you like Florida?" The response was a grunt.

I was at a complete loss. I groped for something, anything, to say. I finally said, "Wasn't she beautiful?"

He knew exactly who I was talking about. The sneer reappeared on his face. He said, "I made love to Mrs. Seid."

I was frozen. I was speechless. I thought the only person I could possibly share this with was my brother, David. How could this magnificent woman with the prematurely grey hair and flawless skin have possibly laid down with a disgusting hair ball like Butchy, never mind letting him into her house? I spotted David in the hallway, welcoming some of his guests to the party. I rushed over to him, grabbed his arm and pulled him away from the door.

"What is the matter with you?" David asked. "Can't you see I'm busy!"

"David," I said, "this is urgent! I was just talking to Butchy and out of nowhere he tells me that he made love to Mrs. Seid!"

David laughed and said, "And you believe him?"

"I don't know. Somehow it definitely had a ring of truth. Why else would he be saying it long after it supposedly happened? It's really difficult to believe that the incredibly lovely Mrs. Seid would even consider him. I'm sure you remember her. Do you think it's possible?"

David laughed again, "She was a pretty one, although I liked the daughter better. I don't know...maybe he fixed her car and didn't charge her?"

The years passed. One day, I was busy working in my office when David called, "Butchy has been very sick. His wife just called and said it's only days. He won't make it."

"Are you going down there?" I asked.

"Unfortunately, I can't. I have a critical meeting in Texas. I'll be in Texas all week."

"What hospital is he at"? I asked.

"He is at Miami General. Why?"

"Because I'm going down there as soon as I hang up from you."

"Good luck," David said.

I raced to the airport. I didn't care what it would cost to buy a ticket without a reservation or the cost of renting a car. I had to know. I just knew he wouldn't lie on his deathbed.

I found my way to the hospital and his room. Butchy's wife, Dora, was sitting by his bedside. Her eyes were red from not sleeping. She thanked me for coming as I walked toward Butchy's bed. Butchy had tubes coming out of everywhere. He looked like he had lost fifty pounds. Once again, I had no idea what to say. I couldn't say, "How are you?".

A floor nurse had spotted my entrance. She came rushing in and said, "Please don't try to talk to him. His situation is very critical."

Butchy looked up. He sneered that old familiar sneer. He motioned to the nurse to hand him some notepaper and pen. Butchy scribbled something down on the paper and, with trembling hands, folded it up and handed it to the nurse. He then touched the nurse's hand holding the note and, with his other hand, pointed at me. The nurse gave me the note. I left.

I didn't open the note until the flight attendant brought me two small bottles of red wine. First, I finished one of the bottles and then, with trembling fingers, I opened the note. It read, "I did and you didn't!!!"

17

Foul Weather Friends

MY SISTER, CHARLOTTE, was quite sick. She knew she was dying, losing her fight with ovarian cancer. She decided to throw herself a party. The party would be in Plano, Texas where her daughter's family lived. All of the invited guests were registered in the same hotel, and most of us seemed to arrive at about the same time. There were quite a few more people than there were automobiles. In order to get everybody to the party hall on time, those with a car were assigned at least one passenger.

My wife, Dana, and I were introduced to my sister's friend, Mandy Press, from the Concord school where my sister taught for the last fifteen years. Mandy appeared to be quite a bit older than my sister, who was eight years older than me. She appeared to be quite frail, fragile even. Mandy was wearing a very drab brown dress that had matching brown buttons all the way up the front. Her dull grey shoes were seriously vintage. They reminded me of the shoes my grammar school teachers wore in what seemed to be a century ago. We exchanged the usual *nice to finally meet you.* Mandy added that Charlotte had told her quite a bit about me.

Mandy said, "She calls you her baby brother, Bobby."

I took her elbow and walked her very carefully to the car, taking very small steps. I held the back door of the car open for Mandy and waited patiently, holding the door open until I was sure her seatbelt was securely fastened. I cautiously closed the door, making sure that she was safely tucked in. I then ran back to the front desk to confirm the directions to the party hall.

We drove off and in less than five minutes, we were lost. We pulled over to the side of the street and by some miracle, there was a police car parked directly across from us. I rolled my window down and called out to the policeman. He came sauntering across the street with a very long flashlight in his hand. When he got to our car, he put his flashlight on and pointed it in my direction.

"What seems to be the problem?" he asked.

I explained that we were from out of town and misdirected.

"You mean you're lost," he said. "Where are you trying to get to?"

"We want to go to the Marriott on Quarim," I said.

"Oh," the policeman said, "I know where that is."

Still pointing his flashlight, he seemed to be looking through the car to see if there were any dead bodies on the car floor or small bags of smack or whatever.

"Just go right at this block. Go two lights, make a right. Go about one quarter of a mile and you will see the Expressway North. Get off at the first exit. It is right there, off the expressway. You can't miss it!"

I said, "Thanks."

I thought, *He said we can't miss it. Ha!* I turned the car to the right as the policeman had directed and said, "I wonder what old Tex would have thought if I had floored the car and squealed the tires? These Dallas police seem a little testy. He sure seemed suspicious of us."

Mandy, sitting in the back seat, laughed and said, "I just don't like the fuckers."

"Excuse me," I said, a bit startled.

"You heard me," she said. "All cops do is spend their days and nights looking for trouble. When trouble comes, they either do the wrong thing or they do nothing. I just don't like the fuckers; never have. Did your sister ever tell you how we met?" Mandy asked.

I said, "Yes, I think you guys were teachers together."

"That shows what you know. I'll tell you how we met. My daughter, Theresa, was in Charlotte's class and Theresa refused to read the book Charlotte had assigned the class. Your sister was bullshit. In fact, she was so pissed that she called me that night to squeal on Theresa. Ha! First, I told Charlotte that she was a squealer and that I didn't like squealers. Then I told her that if my daughter didn't want to read the damn book, she didn't have to. There were plenty of other books for her to read and that reading that book wasn't important."

"What book was it?" I ventured.

"Damned if I remember. Hmm, wait a second. Ah, I'm pretty sure it was *The Prince and The Pauper.*"

"Well, why didn't your daughter want to read it?"

"How should I know?" Mandy almost shouted. "I never asked her. It wasn't my business. I don't know. Maybe she saw the movie? Maybe she read a lousy review of it?"

"What grade was this?" I asked.

"I think it was the eighth grade. Anyway, who cares what grade? I am trying to tell you a damn story and you keep asking stupid questions."

"Sorry," I stammered.

"So anyway, that year ended in a draw. Theresa didn't read the book. I never went to the school. I refused to take any more calls from Charlotte and Theresa didn't get an A. She always got A's. But here comes the best part of the story. At the beginning of the next school year, the very beginning," Mandy emphasized, "all the teachers were called in to a meeting by the principal. The principal announced that a Mrs. Mandy Press was going to be the new School Librarian. Well, you can bet your sister almost shit a brick. What I wouldn't have paid to see her face that day.

Anyway, your sister said to the principal, hoping against hope, I guess – I've never really understood that expression - your sister says, 'Is that Mandy Press? Theresa Press's mother?'

'Yes,' the principal answered. 'Why do you ask?'

'Oh, my G-d! That's terrible! This woman never came to the school conferences and the one time she answered the phone to speak to me about Theresa, she was hostile and undermining.'

"Well," Mandy went on, "you had to know this principal to really understand this story. He was the kind of guy who always asked for your opinion. But when he got it, he, of course, hated it. He had a big sign on his wall, 'My door is always open.' I learned quickly enough what that meant. Ha! It meant you can leave the same way you came in, especially if you don't agree with me. So are you getting the picture, Bobby? Here is your poor sister, shocked and wondering if her school world is collapsing around her. The school she loves to work at is hiring this crazy woman, someone who doesn't even care enough about her own child to discuss the child with her teacher. And now she has gone and done it. She has told the Principal on me.

Remember I told you I had called her a squealer? Your sister's words were out and this very 'open-minded, care what other people think' of a principal is glowering at Charlotte. Well, your poor sister is by now just sitting there wishing she could crawl into the nearest hole when, best of all for Charlotte, at that moment, the school bell rings and the teachers have to go back to their classes. You should hear your sister tell this tale! When she told it to me years later, I thought I was going to pee my pants. You know, of course, we became best of friends. Your sister often says that I'm the best darn librarian she ever met. And coming from your sister, Charlotte, that's a compliment. Anyway, I want to tell you that it is still a draw."

"How so?" I asked.

"That's the last stupid question of yours I'll answer. Well, Theresa is now just about forty years old. She is a teacher at the Concord school, where Charlotte and I were. She still refuses to read or teach *The Prince and The Pauper* and I have yet to teach your sister how to swear properly."

18

Pets with Attitude

I NEVER REALLY understood why people want pets. I certainly don't. Even as a kid, pets couldn't have been further from my mind. The closest I ever came to having a pet was a turtle. Some pet! You can't walk a turtle. Can you imagine trying to put a leash on a turtle?

Years later, we lived in Byfield. My wife, Dana, explained to me that since we lived in such a rural area, it was a must to have a dog. A good size one was also important.

I never asked why, although years later, I did ask myself why I hadn't asked why.

We got an extremely well-bred brown Standard Poodle. She was copper brown. So, of course, we named her Penny.

Penny came with a very large ego and even larger attitude. Penny was sure she was smarter than Dana or me.

Penny was right!

Dana took her to a dog training class. Evidently, the coach told the group to praise their dogs frequently.

However, she said to Dana, "Not that one! She doesn't need praise," the instructor smiled. "I know conceit when I see it."

There was no leash law at that time in Byfield. We would let Penny out early in the morning until we heard from our neighbors that Penny was stealing their children's lunches.

I began to scold Penny. She looked up as if to say, "Oh I suppose you could pass up a salami and cheese with a touch of mustard on a bulkie roll?"

My father-in-law, Aaron, was crazy about Penny. They were very similar in personality. He offered to take Penny off our hands. Before he could finish asking, I was handing him Penny's leash.

Penny looked up at me. "Finally, finally, a home where I'll be properly appreciated."

I was sure she and Aaron went to single bars together.

A few years later, we moved to Lexington. Once again Dana explained to me that it was very important for our children to have a dog. This time, we'd get a smaller dog.

Once again I didn't ask why, although years later I asked myself why didn't I ask why?

We purchased a Westie. All Westies have white fur. We named him Honkie. Honkie was very handsome. Honkie was very bright, but Honkie, too, had attitude. Honkie's attitude was towards women. He didn't like them, especially my two daughters. He was constantly growling at my girls.

One day, I growled back at Honkie, "This is the tenth and last time I'm going to tell you to stop snarling at my daughters."

Honkie, who was very good with numbers, looked up and blinked. "I only counted eight times."

That was it! He was better at math than I was. Time to send him to a home for growling and snarling Westies.

"Enough pets!" I said to Dana.

We went pet-free until recently when our daughter, Rebecca, came home to our house for a stay of four months. Along with Rebecca came two of her dogs. One of them was a Tibetan Spaniel named Toto. The other, a Pug, was named Mookie.

Toto had attitude. He didn't like being a dog. "You should have seen me before. I was gorgeous. I had such a beautiful mane of blond hair. Women loved all six-foot-three of me."

Poor Toto couldn't believe he came back as a dog. His only consolation was that all the women told him how beautiful he was.

Two days after he moved in, I went to Walgreens and bought him his own mirror.

Mookie, on the other hand, was not vain. Mookie had only one concern, and that was food. Mookie was a beggar. It didn't matter how much food he got, he wanted more.

When I ate, he sat close by me. Mookie knew there was a fifty/fifty chance I might drop some crumbs on the floor.

But even if I didn't, he had the perfect face for a beggar. His face was beyond sad. His face was communicating, "Your daughter, Rebecca, doesn't feed me. I know she tells you she feeds me. She doesn't! She's a liar! It's been months since I've had any food."

When I opened the refrigerator door, Mookie looked in it with me. "Please, Please. I don't care how old the food is. Anything at all will do. Please don't throw anything out."

If the homeless and hungry street people could somehow have their faces redone to look like Mookie's, in no time they would become very wealthy. Cars would come to hurtling stops to give them money.

My daughter left. It had been a wonderful treat having Rebecca home. She took the dogs with her.

I could see Dana's eyes saying to me, "How about a very, very small pet? Please, Please."

"ABSOLUTELY NOT! NOT EVEN A TURTLE!" I scream.

19

This Old House

THE YOUNG MAN'S hands were shaking, as he pulled out his checkbook to give us his rental deposit on the house.

"I have one question," he said. "Is this house spooked?" Not a smart question to ask within earshot of our sensitive ghosts.

Unbelievably Dana ventured, "Of course, but they are nice ghosts. They won't bother you if you respect the house."

I've seen people move in my time, but never as fast as this young man. Dana and I were sure we heard the ghosts giggling.

How did all of this happen? I flashed back thirty-five years. Dana, our baby Sarah, our Westie, and myself lived in a NYC apartment on East 54th street. We had a very functional space and best of all, a courtyard. One day, Dana said, "We need a shelf in our kitchen."

Why?" I asked.

"To put stuff on," Dana explained.

"A shelf in our kitchen? They don't deliver shelves in New York. It's not pizza!"

"Have you ever heard of hardware stores?" asked Dana.

"Yes," I noted, "but there aren't any hardware stores in New York. In NYC, nobody tries to fix things themselves. People call the super or somebody that knows how to fix things."

Dana sighed, "On your way to work, there is a hardware store on 49th and Third. Tell them what you want to do. They will sell you everything you need."

I did what I was told and put up a usable shelf that actually held stuff.

Sometime later, Dana woke up, nudged me and said, "We have to move."

"Why?" I went back to sleep.

When I awakened, Dana was waiting. "Because our apartment is too small."

"Do you want me to move out?" I asked.

"We need a bigger place," Dana said.

"Where? All the larger apartments are crazy expensive. We have an incredible bargain here."

"What about checking the burbs. Let's drive out to New Jersey. It will be an adventure," Dana smiled.

"Let's find one of those New Jersey diners that prepare every food known to man and listen to people speak."

"Why do that?" Dana asked.

"For one thing, their menus are fabulous, and for another thing, our kids are going to grow up with whatever accent the area has."

We found a fine-looking Jersey diner, ordered our food and listened to the accent.

"Don't think so," said Dana. "Let's try Long Island." We did. Same results.

"I guess we should go back to Massachusetts where people speak like us."

We drove to Boston and began checking the real estate sections. *Old Colonials only forty miles from Boston and reasonable.*

"Where?"

"Newburyport. Let's go!" Dana was excited.

We drove there and took a deep breath. "Look at these houses! They are palaces!"

We found an agent named Raymond. We were impressed. He was wearing a pinstripe banker's suit along with well-shined black wing-tip shoes. Best of all, he spoke with a New England accent.

He took us from house to house. He had a way with words as he pointed out each house's features.

These old houses welcomed us. Dana and I were sure we heard them saying, "You look like such a lovely young couple. Please, please buy us. Insensitive people tramp through saying they're shocked that we're still standing."

Late that afternoon, Raymond took us to this very old house that dated back to the 1600s. It had been vacant for a long time. Stray cats had lived there. It smelled accordingly.

"Six fireplaces, two with beehive ovens. One fireplace hearth stands almost five feet in height. Many of the rooms have the original beam ceilings. Look at the patina on the wood." Raymond struck a serious pose, "I held this house for you. Your names are on it. This is the last house I'll show you today."

Weeks later we learned through the townies why he was so keen to have us buy that particular house. The day was getting late. His seat at the local tavern was beckoning.

I whispered, "I sense this house is spooked!! It's also way too much work!!"

Dana eyed me. "Why? You put up a shelf in New York City."

20

My Back Stories

TWO VOICES RUMINATED in my head as I drove home.

"*What's wrong with you? I told you that wasn't the best story to audition with.*"

"That's your opinion. I bounced three stories off of three people and they all said this one."

"*Well, you didn't tell it well.*"

"I did okay. Why don't you be quiet for once?"

I was driving home from an audition. I hadn't known there would be an audition. I had thought, when Kevin Brooks called me, that I had been selected as one of the storytellers at Three Apples. Actually, I'd been chosen to audition for the event.

"*When are you going to learn to pick the story yourself? How many times do I have to tell you?*" cried the insulting voice.

When I arrived home, my wife, Dana, greeted me, "How did it go? Tell me where and when?"

"That's not what happened. Remember I said that I was picked to be one of the performers at Bedford's Three Apples. I was wrong. It was just an audition."

"What now?" asked Dana.

"What now! We sit by the phone and wait for their call."

"Well, we don't have much food here, 'Mr. What Now'. Let's eat out," Dana said.

"We have wine and I saw some crackers in the kitchen. I'm not moving until they call. They said they would get back to me soon," I exclaimed!

"What does 'soon' mean?" asked Dana.

"It means we sit here till the phone rings."

"Soon" arrived three days later. I was selected to be a storyteller at "Three Apples."

● ● ●

Quite a few years ago, Dana and I were asked to perform at a ten-year-old's birthday party.

I had the perfect story. It featured fairy godmothers from a long, long time ago.

As I stood in front of those way too cool ten-year-olds, I began, "This was so long ago. There were no cars at the time."

Not one child blinked.

I went on, "There were no planes. There were no radios. No TVs. There were no computers!"

I continued, "There was no baseball, so there were no hot dogs!" Still no reaction from anyone of them.

Finally I said, "No pizza."

Twenty ten-year-olds shouted in unison. "No pizza! No pizza?? What did they eat?"

"Couldn't the fairy godmothers make some toast and put some red sauce on it like my mother does?" shouted one of the children.

I finished the story, but now I had a new story, probably even better than the story I came to tell. Guess what food these kids celebrated the birthday party with?

• • •

It was one of my first performances. I was the feature at Brother Blue's Story Space. I was telling a story I call "The Life Of The Party." In the story, I had recently moved to New York City from Boston and I was getting invited to parties mostly run by women, who worked as editors for various publications. I finally get to the part of the story where I'm at one of these parties when a woman walks in, whom I really want to meet. I ask someone her name. I'm told that it is Domenique. I discover she is a senior editor at Vogue magazine.

I have no idea what I'm going to say to her. I pray she doesn't notice my shaking knees.

I walk over to her, "I saw an interesting foreign film last evening."

"Oh," Domenique impatiently responds, "you may go on! But sum it up succinctly."

I tell this audience that I summed it up with one word; a word I still cannot define.

Standing there in front of this audience of over sixty people, I cannot remember the word!

Later after finishing my monologue, one member of the audience rushes up to me and says, "Brilliant!!"

I'm hoping he means my monologue.

"What?" I ask.

He says, "That pause when you acted like you couldn't remember the word."*

---

* To find out the "word", see p. 99.

21

A Collection of Nothing

DO YOU KNOW what I mean? You know those tomatoes that have been sliced perfectly small. I've only seen them at Mexican restaurants and, of course, sub shops. They had this flashy ad on TV for what they called a ONE-MINUTE SLICER. It's true that it takes only seconds to slice the tomatoes to look just like the Mexican Restaurants' tomatoes. What they don't tell you is how long it takes to clean the ONE-MINUTE SLICER.

Yesterday I asked Dana where the slicer is.

Dana replied, "It's in the basement with your collection that you bought from those ads. Besides, when did you use it last?"

"A while ago," I offered. "But you didn't have to send it to the basement as if it has done something bad. I like having the things I bought where I can see them, just in case."

"Just in case what?" asked Dana. "If you want to see them, they are ALL lined up downstairs in the basement where I put them. Go take a peek. There's the pressure cooker that promised to cook a four-pound roast in twenty five minutes. Remember it took us over two hours putting it together and then reading the directions took another hour. Then there are all the hoses that shrink themselves up that we haven't returned yet. You still haven't found the return address. Anyway, at least I got a giggle out of your expression when you turned one on for the first time and it immediately sprung a leak. You were soaked. You screamed, 'This is the last time I'll call up about one of those ads!' How many more have you called since? I won't ask."

Dana was correct. I don't know what it is, but I can't resist those commercials. I used to be safer. Years ago, those gimmicky ads would only show up on the Late Late Movie that came on at about 11:30 PM. Oh, they were very clever. For the first hour, they would be almost commercial-free and then the last hour, there would be an ad every seven minutes. There would be ads for all sorts of kitchen equipment. The advertisers would demonstrate how beautifully they worked and why one couldn't go another five minutes without owning one. And yes I would find myself staggering to the phone at one-thirty in the morning speaking to a robot and fumbling for my credit card. The best thing about those Late Late Movies is that I rarely stayed up to watch them. But now the problem is that these ads are being shown over and over again on the early evening shows that I watch.

Another reason I find these products irresistible is that they always offer two for the price of one. That way, I can always send one to one of my daughters or a friend that, perhaps, is yearning for a pressure cooker or a one-minute slicer. The cooking utensil ads are by far the hardest to resist. Usually, they are produced and performed by a famous chef who has just invented the newest "must have" cooking tool. These ads generally show the chef cooking something delectable. The chef will go on to say that the new product will not only cook "whatever" quickly, but it will cook it healthier than any other product has since the beginning of time. If that didn't make you rush to the phone, there would always be at least two tasters, literally licking their chops after they were offered a bite.

Dana probably doesn't know about two products that promise to repair anything that's broken. I purchased them from two different companies. One is called Flex Shot; the other is called Flex Soak. Flex shot only comes in one color

Flex soak comes in a multitude of colors. With Flex Shot you can match the color of anything.

Dana cannot possibly know that I will call the 800 number for Wipe New Dutch Glow that swears it will remove all scratches on anything regardless of how deep. I believe it because I saw them do it on TV.

I'll not tell her about the Simonize product that will make my car look "like it just came out of the show room." Why would I mention the all-purpose razor that promises to last at least one year?

Why would I give her an excuse to line them up with the rest of my collection in the basement?

22

WHY MEN ARE SUSPICIOUS OF YOGA

MY SOCIOLOGY PROFESSOR at the extension school asked us to write a paper to describe the emotional differences between men and women. I decided to go to a local sports bar that generally catered to mostly "guy" guys. I took a stool at the bar and tuned in. The more they spoke about sports, the deeper their voices became. Football comments were getting the deepest tones, but basketball, soccer, boxing, even tennis was seriously discussed. There were TV screens everywhere.

A Red Sox game was on. There were lots of high-fives whenever the Red Sox scored a run. Then it happened. One of the guys said that he heard Yoga was a good healthy activity. He also mentioned that it could be quite strenuous. There was silence. Yoga just did not resonate with these guys.

Mostly these guys were eating burgers and fries with lots of ketchup. It occurred to me that if one of these guys mentioned that they had just tried some tofu with brown rice, there would also be silence.

Not too many weeks after my bar adventure, my wife, Dana, and I were driving to Providence when Dana said, "I have a question for you."

Oh, oh! I thought. *I'm caught here in my car. There is no place to hide. I know a trap question when I see it coming.*

"How long would you say that I've been teaching yoga?" asked Dana.

I thought. *No way can I answer this correctly. If I said too few years, it meant I didn't appreciate and value her work. If I said too many years, it meant I didn't appreciate and value her work.*

I took a shot. "Seventeen years?"

"Try twenty-two. And how many times have you come to one of my classes?"

"Not many," I said.

"How about none," Dana retorted.

"Not many is close to none," I said.

"How many times have I come to one of your performances?"

"A lot," I said.

"When are you planning to come to one of my classes?" asked Dana.

"Soon."

"Soon? I may have to look up the definition of soon," she muttered.

Dana teaches classes in many different places. She teaches three classes at the Boston Sports Club, the local "Y", a class at Health Point, and another in Waltham. She also teaches at our Temple once a month. I would go that Friday.

The timing was perfect. This experience would do wonders for my paper along with the bar experience. The Temple class had the fewest people to look foolish in front of.

I entered a dark room. I saw five women sitting silently and not moving. Their knees were pulled forward, held by their hands. I tried to recall. When did I ever see men sit like that?

Dana is speaking in a very soft melodious voice. She is saying, "We will be going on a journey."

I'm thinking, when men go on a journey, they go somewhere.

Soft strange music is playing in the background and these women continue to sit. They are not moving.

Dana then says, "We will take a path."

I'm thinking about guys like myself. They think of a path as something to walk on. These women don't. They think of a path as a way of life.

Dana then began to speak about sharing.

When men talk about sharing, they are usually talking about something substantial like food or drinks. These women are talking about sharing the spirituality of the moment.

Dana then tells her students to caress their legs very gently.

Now when men hear the word caress, they usually aren't thinking of caressing their own legs.

Dana went on, telling her students to stretch their hands down to their toes and stretch each toe.

When men put their fingers to their toes, they are usually checking for lint.

As I look around the room trying my best to fit in, I'm aware that there are candles everywhere. Generally speaking, men don't like candles. They love fires. They will go anywhere for a fire. They will follow fire trucks for miles to see a house on fire. They also love campfires. They especially love barbeque pits. The bigger, the better. They just don't like candles. They don't like their aroma and they definitely don't like the hot wax.

The women are now back in their original position. Dana is talking about how nicely the women have aligned their hips. I'm sitting there trying to find my hips.

Suddenly, the room is full of strange sound. "Ommmmm. Ommmmmmm."

I have no idea what it's about, but I'm terrified. Is this some secret code word women have and they plan to "ommmmmm" me?

That evening, when we got home, Dana asked what I thought of the class.

I responded with the only answer I could muster, "Ommmmmmmmmmm."

23

My Street Has Gone to the Dogs:
Another Street Has Gone Afoul

WHILE DRIVING DOWN my street, I saw a coyote. It was strutting toward my car, making it clear that it would not get out of the way. In fact this coyote went eyeball to eyeball with me as if to say, "What are you looking at, buddy?" I had read that coyotes were shy of humans, but that was before they came East and learned how to read. They definitely knew that Lexington persons leaned liberal and so were generally not gun-toters.

Not many months ago, I was busy on my computer. It was late and I was ready for bed. Just as I was about to close up, a bat flew very close to my head. I quickly climbed the stairs and awakened my wife, Dana.

"We have a bat in the house."

"What am I supposed to do about it?" murmured Dana.

"I'm not going to sleep with a bat in the house. I'll call the police."

The policeman's response was, "What am I supposed to do about it?"

The next day, I called our exterminator and set a date. By the time the exterminator arrived on the scene, the bat had fled.

However, he noted we had a lot of squirrels and chipmunks. "I can get rid of those pests if you want. I'll spread a little fox urine and you'll not see them again."

Two days later, I was looking for my garden shovel in our shed. There in the shed was a very handsome fox looking at me as if to ask, "What are you doing in my villa?" Evidently, the urine was of the female variety.

I had heard that most foxes were afraid of humans. However, I was afraid this particular fox might mistake me for his long-awaited lover.

I called the exterminator.

"We don't exterminate fox," he said.

"You brought him here!" I screamed

"Okay, okay," he yelled back, "but you'll have to live with the chipmunks and squirrels."

I sighted the fox a few more times. He no longer was going into the shed, his villa, but rather slinking and sniffing through my yard. He spotted me and threw me a disgusted look, making it clear that I was far from his fantasy fox.

• • •

The reporter from *The Gazette* walked into the local coffee shop, looked around and said to no one in particular "Does anyone here know anything about a rooster named Rudi?

My paper, if you can believe it, has sent me on assignment to find out all I can about this rooster."

A few heads turned from the counter to check out the reporter. Voices were raised.

"I hate that bird! He thinks he's so smart, but he doesn't even know the time of day. He doesn't care when he cock-a-doodle-doos. Usually, it's the middle of the night."

"He knows alright. He's just a mean-spirited rooster. He couldn't be happier about waking us. I've spotted him after he's awakened us. Meanest grin I've ever seen."

A middle-aged woman commented, "I used to feed him when he came by my shop. I'd save half my sandwich for him. Usually, it was hummus or eggplant. He always ate nicely and seemed to enjoy our luncheons together. One day, I had egg salad. Well, I never! He squawked like I was trying to kill him. Maybe too much mayo? Now, he walks by my store with his beak in the air."

A young man turned to the reporter and said, "Nobody, and I mean nobody, could catch that bird. He's way too smart, but I hear that some character is driving over eight hundred miles with multiple plans to catch that bird."

The reporter smiled and said, "What's your luncheon special today? I hope it's not chicken salad."

24

Ants on a Log

WE WERE EXCITED. We were flying out to L.A. We were going to be there in time for our seven-year-old granddaughter's graduation. Finleigh was graduating from first grade. We knew how proud she was by our last FaceTime with her.

However, before one goes anywhere, one has to pack. Packing is not pretty. The objective should be to take as little as possible. A goal never reached! I know that I need a bag-packing app watching my every article that I place carefully in my suitcase. I need one that will not hesitate to scream, "Are you kidding me? You don't need that! You already have packed seven pairs of underpants. No, you don't need the purple pair. You said you are staying for one week. One week is seven days. We don't pack for your 'just in case.' We pack for seven days! Two pairs of dress pants is more than enough, and one dress shirt." But no such apps were available. When I handed my bag to the Avis shuttle driver, she definitely had the right to holler, "Are you trying to kill me?"

We arrived on Thursday evening at the hotel L.A. time, which was about 11:00 P.M. Boston time was 2:00 A.M. Still, we were at Finleigh's school the next morning at 9:30. There would be playtime for the children and potluck. I was very hungry, but I had to remind myself that this would be California food. There was a huge platter of hummus. I have issues with chickpeas, so not for me. What on earth is on the next platter? I recognize the celery, but what is it possibly stuffed with? How to best describe it? It was brownish color with little black dots on top of the brown spread.

I inquired, "What is that?" as I pointed hesitatingly at the celery with brown stuffing.

"Oh, that's organic peanut butter and the dots are raisins," smiled Finleigh.

"What's that called?" I asked.

"It's called Ants on a Log," Finleigh answered, as if to say, "I've got a lot to teach you, Grandpa."

"Sounds delicious, especially the ants parts," I offered.

Anyway, I'm a nut for peanut butter. I wondered about the organic. What would make this peanut butter more organic than the no-sodium brand I buy? But I already had asked enough stupid questions. Now I thought for a few seconds about the raisins. I'm not crazy about raisins. However as mentioned before, I was very hungry. I took one stalk. *Not bad*. I reached for two more. By the time they closed the brunch, I had eaten half the platter. No one else had any interest in the Ants. They were all hummus people. When we get home, I'll bring this specialty to our next party. I can't wait till they ask, "What do you call this?"

The rest of the week was spent picking up Finleigh from her various activities. Each evening Finleigh insisted on ten jokes.

My first favorite was the teacher asks Johnny, "How do you spell the country called Colombia?"

Johnny spells it K-o-l-u-m-b-i-a.

"Incorrect," says the teacher.

Johnny replies, "But you asked how I spell it."

My second favorite was Johnny is asked if he says his prayers before dinner.

Johnny responds, "No, my mom is a great cook."

Finleigh sighed, "Grandpa, did you say your prayers before you ate the Ants on a Log?"

Soon it was time to pack again. Now I definitely could use a packing app. What could be more embarrassing than the hotel calling me and asking if I had left a pair of purple underpants in the drawer?

IV

The World and Robert Meet

25

Life of the party

WHEN I WAS four, I was invited to my best friend Howard's birthday party. My mother walked me to his house. She straightened my cap and my tie. "Now I expect you will be my very best Bobby."

"I promise, Mummy."

The party was lots of fun. We played marbles. We had cake and ice cream. We all clapped as Howard blew out the candles.

It was now time for Howard to open his presents. There were many, many presents. In fact, in my mind, too many for Howard and none for me.

With the opened presents piled higher than Howard, I let out a scream, "The next one is mine. Howard has enough presents. I don't have any. I want one."

Howard's mother looked down at me, "It's Howard's birthday. All of the presents are Howard's."

"No, no, no! I want that one."

I didn't let up. I continued to screech, "That one is MINE!! It's MINE!"

Howard's mother called my mother. "Bobby is raising a ruckus. Come get him!"

My embarrassed mother picked me up. I didn't stop. "I wanted that one."

Although I was only four, my behavior at Howard's party got me a reputation. I no longer was invited to parties. Evidently, whenever my name was mentioned, someone would say, "Uh, uh, not him. He'll raise a ruckus. Remember him at Howard's party? Wanting Howard's presents? He's big trouble."

That dark cloud stayed over me through Bar Mitzvah's and Confirmations to which I was never invited. Worst of all, when the people I thought of as friends began sending out wedding invitations, I did not receive one.

I was twenty years old. The only party I had ever gone to was Howard's four-year-old birthday party.

It was time to leave town. I had no choice. I packed my bags and moved to Manhattan, two hundred and ten miles from Howard's house. I knew no one there and best of all, no one knew me.

I very quickly made friends with a group of women who lived in my apartment building. It seemed most of them were editors working for various magazines.

They told me that every Friday night there was a party at somebody's apartment.

"Hey why don't you come tonight?" asked Sue. "I'll introduce you to all my friends. It will be a blast."

Finally, I was going to a party.

I learned the rules quickly. Best to speak only three or four minutes to anyone and then move on. Since I could never figure out what to say, three minutes was more than enough.

One evening as I was busy mingling, *she* walked in. I was transfixed. "Do you know her?" I asked one of the guys.

"Yeah, that's Domenique. She's a senior editor at Cosmos. She eats guys like you and spits them out for fun."

Smitten, I ignored him. I walked over to Domenique. I smiled. She didn't.

She said, "Yes?"

"I saw this wonderful Fellini movie last night."

She looked at me with little interest, "Sum it up succinctly, please!"

I used a word I had never used before or since. I still have no idea what it means. "Existential," I stammered.

Domenique glared at me and stomped off.

Happily for me, I met Dana, my wife to be. Dana had never attended a party. Her dad had been a "wannabe" polo player. He decided Dana would fulfill his dreams. As soon as Dana was old enough to walk, he took her for riding lessons and then polo lessons. Dana had no time for parties.

Since I'd been to NYC parties, I decided I would show Dana the ropes.

Both of us were in the design business. As a result, we subscribed to Women's Wear Daily. Each week we would peruse our copy and immediately turn to the photo-op page. Each week there would be photos of beautiful people gazing into one another's eyes. Underneath the photo, the copy always read, "Anybody who is Anybody attended this party." It didn't matter to us that none of these people knew us. What hurt was that we hadn't been invited.

Time to leave Manhattan. We went back to Massachusetts. We settled in Newburyport about forty-five miles north of Howard's home. Newburyport was a party town. There were at least two parties every weekend. Generally, there was quite a bit of drinking, smoking and music. Soon, Dana and I felt party-savvy.

In fact, the first party invitation was from a doctor who had just remarried. He had a new beautiful house, a heated pool, and a young wife to celebrate. When we arrived, like all the other guests, we were sweltering from the heat. However, the doctor announced that the pool was "off limits". No sooner did he say that than he pushed his ex-college roommate into the pool. The cry went out. Everybody jumped into the pool. Minutes later, all the swimmers disrobed. Soon, everyone was naked.

Dana quietly said, "I don't like the way this party is going. I'm heading home. I've got some laundry to finish."

I looked over at the pool and said, "I think I'll stay here. I want to make sure that things don't get way too out of hand."

One Saturday morning we ran into a party regular. "See you at Steve's tonight?"

"We're going to Bill's," I said.

It was obvious by his expression that we were going to the 'B' party because we had not been invited to the 'A' party.

Time to move! Lexington was next. The Lexington parties were very different from the Newburyport parties. There was little drinking and absolutely no smoking. Mostly, conversations centered around their children, all of whom, it seemed at age thirteen or fourteen, were getting early admission to MIT or Harvard.

Our kids were home watching "I Love Lucy" reruns.

Now, we're home altogether watching reruns. We don't go to parties! We don't have to move again.

26

Losing My Cool

I GREW UP in Dorchester, Massachusetts. We wanted more than anything to be cool, mostly because we weren't. If cool were Texas, we were Tokyo.

I moved to Manhattan in my early twenties and realized very quickly I'd better be at least semi-cool to survive in Manhattan. I had a very blond girlfriend. I had a job. I had my own apartment and a tiny swagger to go with all of this. I could sense a smidgeon of cool taking hold.

Every Saturday, I would go to the Bronx office where I worked during the week. I did this to impress my bosses with my sense of purpose. I also would pick up my clothes at the dry cleaners. In order to get to the dry cleaners, I had to pass a Jewish deli. As I passed by, I could smell the aroma of half sour pickles, smoked salmon, corned beef, an aroma that could only come from a truly Jewish deli.

Saturday afternoon used to be an event at my Dad's apartment in Dorchester. He would bring home bagels, smoked salmon, cream cheese and corned beef. I longed for something similar in NYC.

However, the deli was no place to buy for just one person. My girlfriend said she hated deli. She had said many times that she would never go to a place that displayed pickled tongue as an edible food.

One Saturday I could no longer resist. I could not handle the aroma any longer. I had to get my courage up and go into this deli.

I waited in a long line where I was assigned a number to assure my turn. Finally my turn came. The older man behind the glass counter seemed to be very tired. Our eyes met. It was very apparent by his glare that he did not like the look of me. I mustered up all of my courage and said, "I'll have about 30 cents worth of smoked salmon."

He looked at me as if I were speaking in a foreign tongue, which actually, in this deli, I was. He said, "We don't have smoked salmon here, sonny boy. We have *lox!*"

After he sliced a very tiny piece, he said, "It's a little over. Is that okay?"

I nodded and said, "I'll also have about 20 cents worth of cream cheese."

He cut a slab of cream cheese, weighed it and said, "It's a little under. Is that okay?"

Again I nodded. "I notice your potato salad and coleslaw are both 29 cents a pound. Could you mix the two in one container?"

He made a point of showing me the scooper he would normally use and took out a teaspoon, which he proceeded to wave threateningly at me. He very slowly and carefully measured out the slaw and potato salad into one container.

I could feel my cool slipping rapidly away. Quietly I said, "I'll have one bagel please."

He went over to the cash register and glowered, "Eighty-six cents, sonny boy." Then in an even louder voice, he yelled, "*What? Are you having a party?*"

I was sure he could be heard all the way into Manhattan. As I slunk past the long line that had been waiting behind me, I knew in that moment the "cool" I had so carefully acquired in NYC was completely gone.

Although I got a new girlfriend who adored deli, it took many years of serious therapy to regain enough cool to re-enter that deli in the Bronx.

27

The Next Time Someone Tells Me
They're a Witch, I'll Believe It!

I HAD EVERY reason to be horrified. The pilot had just announced that we had lost our brakes and that we would have to land at Dulles Airport rather than Boston. He explained that Dulles had the longest runway on the east coast.

I had more reason than anybody else on that plane to be horrified. I knew that I would be responsible for all my fellow passengers getting killed.

You see, about two years before boarding this flight, I had been in charge of sales and design for a boot manufacturing company. The top boss of the company seemed to go out of his way to make things difficult for my division and me. To say that Ray didn't like me would be a gross understatement. In fact, he hated me. Phil had been working for me for approximately four years. Phil was acutely aware of the

friction between Ray and me, and seemed to take great pleasure in discussing Ray's quirks with me. I, of course, would
respond with great passion, in agreement with everything
Phil said about Ray. What I didn't know was that Phil was
calling Ray every Sunday evening to tell him what I'd said.

Twice a year we were obliged to show our products at a
convention that was usually held in a hotel in New York City.
These shows generally lasted three or four days, and they
were quite grueling. We were on our feet most of the day
and spoke incessantly about our products to any potential
customer willing to listen.

At the end of the day, it was customary for us to try and
relax with some light food and heavy alcohol. Phil's wife,
Bernice, considered it a treat to visit us after she had finished her shopping for the day.

I thought she was a bit peculiar in that she seemed to
take great delight in telling us about her fights with Phil.
Bernice actually told us that upon at least one occasion she
had become so frustrated with Phil that she decked him with
a punch to the nose. I looked over at Phil to see how he was
taking this. He pointed to his nose, showing us where Bernice
had landed her last blow. I also noticed that Phil was wearing
a simpering smile as his beloved Bernice told her tale.

Bernice seemed to take even more delight in sidling
up to me and relating what should have been confidential
between Phil and her.

One evening after most of us had had more than a couple of drinks, Bernice came close enough to me to whisper
in my ear, "I'm a witch."

I think she could tell from the expression on my face that I didn't take what she had just said seriously.

She moved even closer, still whispering, "I know you don't believe me but I am a witch. I've proven it to many people. I hope I never have to prove it to you!"

The inevitable confrontation finally came between Ray and me. Ray called me into his office and said, "I know some of the remarks you've made about me. I want you gone!!"

Shortly thereafter, I went to work for a competitor. A year passed and one of my customers decided to throw a massive party to celebrate a brand-new building that he had built to house his many employees. There was food and drink everywhere. I was having a wonderful time, laughing and joking with old friends and some new ones.

Then I saw Phil standing in a corner looking around. I intended to do everything to avoid him, but he spotted me and came over. He was still wearing that simpering grin. "I hear great things about you," he said.

I lost it. I could not contain my fury. "You miserable floor flusher. You pathetic liar. You sanctimonious creep. You, whose wife owns your balls, get out of my sight."

To my surprise, he crept away. I saw him make his way to a phone booth, no doubt, to call his wife and report what I had said.

This all came back to me as the flight attendant insisted that our seats be erect, as if this might save us. The entire conversation with Bernice about her being a witch and hoping she'd never have to prove it to me came back to me, word for bloody word. I had to go and lose it to that worm

Phil and now all these people were going to die because of it and I would never see my wife and kids again. The rosary beads were out. People were sobbing. Even people who looked Jewish were crossing themselves. I looked down at the runway. There were fire engines everywhere. The runway was smothered in foam. I did this!

The plane descended. You could actually hear people holding their breath. The plane landed, slid a bit, then came to a complete stop. The pilot announced that the brakes were fine. The alarm was caused by a breakdown in his instrument panel.

I heard some of the passengers, who had just put away their rosary beads, say, "Damn. I'm going to miss my connection in Boston."

My thoughts were on finding the nearest phone to call Bernice and thank her for only giving me a warning.

28

"Great Expectations"

WHEN SOMEONE TELLS me how good I look, I frequently say that the person *must have very low expectations*. I believe low expectations are the key to a happier life.

After watching the first of the 2016 Presidential debates, I definitely had extremely low expectations for the third and, thank goodness, the last one. I even had very low expectations regarding the pundits. I watched the same vice-presidential debate they did. CNBC, which tends to favor the left, declared Mike Pence the winner. Mr. Pence sat there for ninety minutes and denied statements that all of America had heard. Tim Kaine disappointed his supporters. He acted like a fifth grader who couldn't contain himself. There was no winner. Besides, what does a winner win?

My wife Dana's mother lives in a senior community. Now, what can your expectations be regarding the food that is served daily to over two hundred persons? Fair at best. Right? Wrong! It was very good. Was it really very good or were my expectations very low? In any case, I walked away with a happy belly.

I've never gone to a five-star restaurant that met my expectations. Actually, the opposite is true. For instance, when I go to a restaurant like the Ninety-Nine, it's always better than I expected. So is McDonald's. (Please don't tell anyone I said that).

Why let this perspective pertain only to food? It sounds like a perfect recipe for life.

Sports fans know this better than anybody. The lower their expectations are for their favorite team, the better chance they have of staying sane. They need to give up the idea that they may have anything to do with the outcome. Some people believe a particular outfit that they wear will help their team win. It *probably* won't! Some believe a certain seat and manner of sitting will influence the game. It *probably* won't! I once visited a friend who was standing on his head trying to watch a football game.

"Why are you standing on your head?" I asked.

"I have a sizable bet on the game and this almost always works."

It didn't.

Just about every day, I read the Boston Globe's two love columns. The writers usually want to know what they did wrong and what they can do to change things. My answer is invariably *nothing*. Having expectations of changing another human being is the ultimate conceit.

The love columnists usually give advice that is long and sensitive, but meaningless. Not true of other readers who leave comments like, "Forget about it!" which is another way of saying "Lower your expectations! Count your blessings! You missed that bullet!"

The stock market analysts are constantly talking about expectations. Nothing could be more absurd, except when we are told that the analysts hate uncertainty. Those two words should be morphed into one. How can anyone live in this world and have any kind of expectation close to certainty?

Some of us believe when we make statements that most people will agree with what we have said. Wrong! It's much better to have low expectations, especially with our significant others. I frequently begin my monologues by asking audiences "What's the sexiest thing your significant other can say to you?" The answer is, invariably, "You are right dear."

If you keep your expectations low, you will not be disappointed that you don't hear, "You are right, dear." very often.

29
Gawkers

I WAS WAITING for my car to be brought up. I was at a parking garage on 34th and 5th Avenue. A woman, who at the time I thought of as quite elderly, was gawking at me.

Finally, I glanced at her and said, "Why are you staring at me?"

"I saw you last night on TV. You were wonderful!"

"Really? What was I doing?"

"You were soooo funny. I couldn't stop laughing." "Do you know my name?"

"No, but I never forget a face."

Usually it was the other way in NYC. Usually I was the gawker. I was on 5th Avenue facing Central Park somewhere in the high nineties. Suddenly there was something wrong. I wasn't sure what it was. I stopped. I wanted to know what was going on. I realized NYC had gone quiet; a quiet I had never experienced before in the city.

I looked around. Nothing was moving. Everything had stopped. Then I saw her. It was Jacqueline Kennedy crossing 5th Avenue. She was walking from the east side to the west side of the avenue. She had a smile on her face that lit up the street.

I had heard the expression that a beautiful woman could stop traffic, but I had never seen it before I saw Jacqueline Kennedy cross 5th Avenue. And there I was gawking.

When I was very young, my friend Steve's parents bought a TV. There wasn't much to watch then. Sometimes we even watched test patterns.

Our favorite show starred Uncle Milty, a.k.a. Milton Berle. We were glued to the set. We thought everything he did was hysterical. Almost every week everything was the same. The jokes. The costumes. We didn't care.

Many years later, I was at a traffic light in NYC. I was watching the pedestrians rushing by. Could that person be Milton Berle? He looked over towards me. He smiled that one and only Uncle Milty smile. He reached in his pocket and took out a toupee. He placed it on his head and smiled triumphantly at me. He knew exactly what I was thinking. There I was sitting in my car gawking at Uncle Milty.

One of my favorite sports books was David Halberstam's *The Summer of '49*. It was mostly about the year the Red Sox lost the pennant to the Yankees on the final day of the season. A great book about a sensitive subject. Halberstam liked to digress. One of his digressions was to write about Earl Wilson, a black pitcher who won eighteen games for the Red Sox in 1964.

Earl Wilson was the first ball player to hire a lawyer to negotiate his salary. He was the second black player to play for the Red Sox. Wilson was not happy with his salary, but he was terrified of negotiating with management. The Red Sox in those days were not known for their color blindness. He discussed his situation with his roommate, who facetiously said, "Why not hire a lawyer?"

Earl Wilson proceeded to hire Robert Wolf. At that time Robert Wolf was a tort lawyer.

Quite a few years later, I was on a plane returning to Boston. In the seat next to me, was Robert Wolf. After hearing about Robert's offices around the world, his dinners with Larry Byrd, etc., I finally got to tell him about reading about him and Earl Wilson. I pretty much quoted the book.

Robert responded, "Nothing like that!"

He then told me his version in lawyerese. To my ears it was the same story. Since he was now a famous Sports Lawyer, he might have deserved a half gawk; but sitting next to him, even a half gawk was not possible

Then there was a trip to Shanghai. The first leg was from Boston to Los Angeles. Across from me in the first-class aisle was Joan Rivers. I had first class status due to my frequent trips to China. Joan was with her dog, her assistant, and a Grace Kelly biography.

Her assistant came over to me and said, "Should Joan know you?"

I explained I was not in the Biz. I asked if Joan were enjoying the book. The assistant said that according to the book, Grace had had more beaus than Joan had funny jokes. I thought, *not too hard.*

I didn't gawk until later when I saw that Joan's husband had gotten the rare privilege of visiting Joan and their dog, although he was seated in coach.

I was picking up my luggage at LAX. A man who had been gawking at me approached with his son. "I'd like your autograph for my son."

"What name should I put down?" I asked.

"What are you? A wise guy?! I saw your last movie. You were awful and so was the movie!"

30

Hugging May Appear Simple:
It's Not!

I GUESS MOST sane persons have not given much thought to hugging. I have. I believe that doesn't mean I'm not sane. It just means I've had a strong curiosity about hugging and huggers for a very long time.

I've tried quite hard to analyze what makes a good hugger and what doesn't.

I know body size has a lot do with it. For instance I believe it's better to be taller than shorter when you are trying to hug someone. It's easier to reach down than up in the process of hugging. Persons who carry some body weight tend to be better at hugging than those who don't.

You also have to be a sincere hugger. I believe even the slightest sign of insincerity in a hug will be detected instantaneously.

Of course, there are hugging methods. There is the one-handed hug. This is not really a hug. It's a hug that says, "I'm sort of glad to see you."

How long the hug lasts is very important. It should be long enough to convey a message.

But as a hugger, you are not in this alone. You are always taking a chance when you reach out to hug. It could be devastating if the other person does not want you to hug them. Worse if you just saw them coming from a major hug with someone else.

Hugging may appear to be simple, but it's not! For years I believed women were thought of - with good reason - as better huggers than men. However, I think men are coming on strong, especially younger men.

I notice that younger men are ready to hug at any sign of a person entering their space. This younger generation seems to have been born with good hugging instincts. They seem to intuitively understand how best to hug a male friend and how best to hug a female friend; even better, how to hug someone who is more than a friend.

I think my curiosity comes from believing myself to be a very poor hugger. The family that helped to raise me did not hug. My friends where I grew up definitely did not hug. I attended an all-boys' school and in those days, if we were spotted hugging one of our classmates, we stood the risk of immediate expulsion.

Hugging is like anything. It takes practice. But that's the catch. It's almost an impossible art to practice.

If you aren't very good at, say tennis or golf, it's not very difficult to find someone to practice with. You can usually go somewhere where tennis is played and find someone of similar ability. This is not true of hugging. I don't know of any gyms that feature hugging classes.

Another serious problem with hugging is nervousness. A certain nervousness or anxiety in sports can work for you. It can help with that competitive edge. But as a hugger, your best approach is cool. Nervousness tends to stiffen the entire body. Body stiffness is definitely a hugging detraction.

I've also had some really un-cool hugging moments. There was the time I had my body totally prepped to hug a woman I was sure I knew. I was wrong.

I whispered, "Sorry. I thought you were somebody else."

She looked at me and said, "Who did you think I was?"

She walked away. I hoped it wasn't a wasted hug.

I checked with Amazon. Sure enough, they had an array of hugging robots. They came in different shapes and sizes. They were also generational, as in young huggers and older huggers.

I went to Yelp. The comments were that the young hugging robots were very good at it, but took themselves too seriously. It seemed that most Yelpers were liking the older robots best, mostly for their cushiness.

I went with the oldest, cushiest female robot. So far I haven't had one disappointing morning.

31

There Are Smiles and Then There Are Smiles

SMILE THOUGH YOUR *heart is achin'. Smile even though it's breaking.*

A few months ago, I wrote a piece on hugging. It not only got me quite a few hugs, it got a lot of comments. Of course, they are all favorable. I plug my ears for any others.

I'm curious what smiles will bring. To me there is a strong relationship between hugging and smiling.

For one thing I'm not particularly good at either. As with huggers there are the natural born smilers. There are the quick study smilers. Then there are the others. I'm definitely one of the others.

I'm never sure if a smile could get me into trouble. For instance if I were to be walking in downtown Lexington, Massachusetts, where I live, and I smiled at all of the people going in the other direction, I'd be put away or arrested!

Women might interpret it as a "come on." Who knows what men might think?

What puzzles me is what if my wife Dana were to do the exact same thing? I am sure she would be greeted with happy, glowing smiles from all genders.

Worse if any of her passers-by were to run into me at a later time, I would hear "What a lovely smile Dana has."

In truth, I have even more issues with Dana's smiles. I've witnessed her meeting one of her friends or even an acquaintance. I watch carefully as they both smile at each other. Then out of nowhere, they'll both break into real, genuine laughter.

"What is that about?!" I cry.

Dana simply smiles at me and says, "If you don't get it, you don't get it!"

I'm thinking most guys I know do not greet each other with big smiles never mind, joyous laughter. She's right, I don't get it!

I'm not ready to quit. I say to Dana, "Okay, I get the *happy to see you* smiles, but nobody spoke! What is so funny? If nobody said anything, why on earth are you laughing?"

Dana looks at me sadly, shakes her head and says, "You really *just* don't get it."

She's right. Guys laugh when somebody says something funny, but not until...

Light up your face with gladness. Hide every trace of sadness.

Kayla Tausche is on various segments of CNBC, but mostly in the AM. Her smile radiates into my bedroom or wherever I'm watching from. She could be discussing a large merger or a significant bankruptcy. It matters not! Kayla will be smiling. Oh, my goodness, don't tell anyone, I'm actually smiling back at her.

I'm wondering if they ask these smiley women to smile, even while covering horrific scenes of death and carnage. *That's the time you must keep on trying. Smile. What's the use of crying?*

In my case I have my most smile troubles when someone is taking photos. Being told to say *cheese* doesn't help. Nothing does. I'm always anxious to see the photos and when I see my glowering self, I mutter, "What did you expect?"

Then there are the polls. Where did Hillary's new smiley face come from? Doesn't she know what she might be getting herself into? Hillary has been there!

Who would want to wake up to that on their plate, especially at 3 A.M.? If it were I, I'd quote William Buckley Jr. when he ran for mayor of NYC, "If elected, I'll demand a recount!!" I wouldn't be smiling; neither should Hillary.

And then there is the Donald Trump smile. There has to be a better word than smile to define it. Whatever it is, it could eat you for breakfast. I'm not smiling back at The Donald.

There are smiles and there are smiles

"You'll find life is still worthwhile if you just smile."

32

TV and Me

WHEN PEOPLE ASK if I watch much TV, I always reply, "Rarely."

I'm a liar! I'm an addict! I have five televisions in my house. If my wife, Dana, allowed it, I'd put them in the bathrooms.

I make it my business to watch "Mad Money" every night. The same edition is on three times daily. I still record it. The show consists of one person, Jim Cramer. Jim is a unique character. Jim is a stock tout. He's very colorful. People call to inquire about their favorite stock. No matter how obscure the stock, Jim most always offers an opinion. If he doesn't like the stock, he presses a button and something starts to yell, "Sell, Sell, Sell!" If Jim likes the stock, he presses another button that yells, "Buy, Buy, Buy!" I find myself dialoguing with the show, but not in a sane way. I hear myself yelling at the tube, "That's not what you said last week! Last week, you said, "Sell" and now that the company's CEO is there, you are screaming, "Buy." Part of me wishes Jim would go off the air waves and free me.

I'm also mesmerized by a show called "Shark Tank." The concept is brilliant. Entrepreneurs present their product to a panel of billionaires. They ask for money in exchange for equity in their business. If I hadn't sold my business, I would have appeared on the show. There are always five panelists. Some alternate. However Kevin O'Leary is always there. He is very witty. He can be very cruel.

When he's not impressed by a presenter, he tells them, "You are dead to me!"

He openly states that he is there for one reason, "Money!"

The other panelists refer to him as the vulture. When he offers a proposal, one of the other panelists will shout, "Next, he'll want your grandchildren."

The other evening a southern woman told Kevin she had her eye on him.

Panelist Barbara Corcoran exclaimed, "What could you possibly see in him?"

Kevin did not raise an eyebrow. He doesn't care. I really like that. He calls himself "Mr. Wonderful." He believes it! I'm absolutely sure Kevin would have bought into my ideas.

This television mania is not new. I began watching TV even before my family bought a television. My neighbor and friend, Steve, had a television. Steve's parents were never home. This allowed Steve and I to watch endlessly. Our favorite show was Milton Berle, or "Uncle Milty" to us. In retrospect Uncle Milty was sort of an unctuous character. Cross-dressing and telling awful jokes filled the hour.

We didn't care. We loved Milton Berle. We even loved the character who did the Texaco commercial. I remember how he rolled up his sleeves and told America why it was critical that we buy our gasoline from Texaco. Steve and I could not get enough! Sometimes we actually watched test patterns.

My parents finally purchased a television. They were hesitant. They were concerned it would interfere with my school work. I assured them that it was not a problem. However, I don't think I ever opened a school book from the day the box arrived.

My mother and I had a routine. We would go to the Mount Bowdoin library situated next to a Brigham's. My mother would select at least five books and off to Brigham's for ice cream. As soon as we returned home, we put the TV on. My mother would then pick up her knitting needles and one of her books. My job was to select a show. It was easy. If it were Wednesday, it would be "Kraft Theatre." Thursday, "Playhouse Ninety."

Whenever a commercial came on, my mother would ask, "Is the show over?"

"Not yet," I would reply.

My mother no longer asked about my homework.

Weekends were special. My dad would be home with us. Friday nights featured, "I Remember Mama," "The Goldbergs," all preceded by Eddie Fisher at 7:00 and Perry Como at 7:30. The three of us were glued to the television. My mother continued to knit but not read. She was too busy arguing with my father about the merits of each show. Saturday was "Your Show of Shows" with Sid Caesar,

Carl Reiner, and Imogene Coca. Among the writers were Neil Simon, Woody Allen, and Mel Brooks to mention a few. Most weeks, they interviewed "The 2000-Year-Old Man." He had met everybody and had a funny comment about everybody.

Sid Caesar performed a skit where he had a flat tire.

He'd be walking to the service station thinking all the terrible things the owner would say when he would ask to borrow a jack. When Sid arrived at the station, he would shout, "Keep your damn jack!"

We loved "Your Show of Shows." Somehow we know this was a very special television moment.

Regardless, I'm still an addict!

33

Ads That Don't Add Up

MY PILLOW: "IT'S guaranteed to be the most comfortable pillow you'll ever own." That's an interesting guarantee. Is it guaranteed to be more comfortable than the pillow I'm presumably sleeping on now, or more comfortable than any one of those I haven't even purchased yet? This character is in my face screaming about his pillow every time I turn on my TV. There is even a sixty-day guarantee. What could go wrong with a pillow? I never heard of a pillow breaking. Also, an offer of a five-year warranty is listed in their ads. A five-year warranty for a pillow! Warranty for what? At the end of five-years, can you imagine calling up this pillow company and demanding a refund?

Have you seen the ad for an asthma medication that shows a big brown bear following an asthmatic couple everywhere they go? Even though the bear is quite large, they don't seem to notice it. The worst part of this situation is that the bear ends up at the foot of their bed when they go off to sleep at night. Since this couple barely notices the bear during the day, they never consider feeding it. It's certainly likely that the bear could wake up very hungry in the middle of the night. Most bears don't know how to cook. I also presume bears know very little about kitchen appliances like refrigerators. Usually they grab whatever is closest to them and begin gorging. They probably don't even require napkins. I'm sure somewhere there is a connection between this very large bear and asthma. I happen to have asthma. However I surely will continue to use my inhaler in preference to having a bear sleep at the foot of my bed. It is noticeable that this medication does not list any side effects. I would believe that this bear is one serious side effect.

Another ad that puzzles me is a particular shirt ad. This cool-looking guy is advertising a shirt that he has patented. It's worn outside your pants, rather than being tucked in. He says he has an 'exclusive' patent on this shirt. He certainly has a very 'exclusive' price on the shirt. I can't imagine how this got by the patent committee. Who hasn't untucked their shirt? I can just hear the dialogue at the patent board. "Hey Frank, look at this shirt! Did you ever see anything like this? It can be worn outside your pants! Wow, what a great idea!!"

Then there is this Subaru ad. It portrays a shaggy-looking grandfather and his grandson heading towards the ocean.

The grandson asks his grandpa, "Did you tell grandma that we were going fishing?"

The grandfather responds incoherently. I'm not sure of his reply.

The scene then flashes to both of them. They are shown picking up their surfboards and gliding into the water. What does this have to do with buying a Subaru? Nothing! But it caught my attention enough to gag when the ad informs me *Love is a Subaru.*

I have to confess, I bought the pillow! I didn't feel any difference. I'm demanding a refund! I'll put the bear in my Subaru. I'll drive to the pillow's office. Since most bears don't wear pants, he can't untuck his shirt. Still I bet with the bear at my side, I'll get my refund!

34

What Do Men and Women Really Want?

A CARTOON SHOWS a husband saying to his wife, "Can you think of a better way to celebrate our anniversary than watching the World Series?"

Interesting question for a man to ask his wife, though it's doubtful she thought it interesting. There are differences between the way men and women look at things. Some show up in our likes and dislikes.

I don't believe I've seen too many women sitting alone at a Dunkin Donuts. Starbucks, yes. On the other hand, I can't remember seeing many men eating by themselves at Panera's.

I'm always surprised when I hear about new trends that get me thinking as to what men and women really want. I had always presumed the point of marriage or being with someone meant just that—*being with someone*. Anyway, according to what I'm now reading, I was wrong.

Married women are putting up sheds in their backyards. She Sheds. More like mini homes. Why? Home Depot and Lowe's are on top of it. Their ads cry out, "How to get away from it all in your own backyard!" And who or what is the *all*?

These sheds are not cheap and they are getting furnished with girlie stuff. It's very clear that most guys will not feel comfortable in these sheds if, in fact, they were welcome, which they are not.

There is currently much copy coming out on She Sheds. There are magazine articles and even books on how to furnish them. Ideas such as returning to what you enjoyed doing as a child are plentiful. If you could see into these sheds, you are apt to see women jumping rope or just sitting with multiple crayons and coloring books. What you won't see is dishwashers, mops, and scrub brushes.

You will see chocolate, a mountain of chocolate. And what goes better with chocolate in a She Shed than a mountain of books? Pillows will be scattered everywhere. Candles will be glowing.

Just the word *shed* says a lot.

Men, on the other hand, have caves. They are called Man Caves. The definition of cave is usually a large underground chamber. These caves are not likely to be underground. They are likely to have a pool table, a dart board, a huge television screen, and a bar with stools. Caves frequently have a dank aroma.

If the guys decide, like the women did, to bring back some of their youth, a password will be needed to enter these chambers. It won't be *open sesame*. One Man Cave used the following password: Ndu$$$$$46Letmein. Attached was a warning: *if forgotten, there will be no new password issued! You will not gain entrance to this Cave! FORGET YOUR PASSWORD, FORGET ABOUT US!*

Small refrigerators harboring beer, cheese, and salami are prerequisites. There will not be any chocolate or candles; maybe one pillow. After visiting a few of these caves, I noted golf putting greens in at least two of them. One of them had a voice shouting compliments. Whenever the golf ball kerplunked into the cup, I overheard, "That was a hole in one! You are truly one of the great putters."

Is this what men and women really want?

35

Embarrassing Duets

"HELLO! HAVEN'T YOU left yet?" my wife Dana called down from the bedroom.

"No, not yet. Why?" I yelled back from the kitchen. "Don't forget you have to buy bathroom tissues for both our house and the office. Both places are cleaned out. Remember to get the soft ones, and hurry back! We want to go to Maine this afternoon."

What? Did she think that I was going to ask for that new macho toilet paper Costco was promoting? The one that feels like sandpaper on one side. They advertised it as the ultimate cleanser. I'll bet it is.

I arrived at Costco early. There weren't a lot of people in the store. Remembering what Dana had instructed, I headed directly to the paper aisle, feeling good that at least some part of my memory was still intact. I'd get this done in no time, I thought.

I picked up two humongous packages of bathroom tissues and juggled them into my cart. Each package contained thirty-six rolls. Imagine if I were at the Stop and Shop and purchased seventy-two rolls of non-packaged bathroom tissues? I can only guess what other shoppers would think looking at my cart.

And people do look at my cart full of bathroom tissue, like they're asking themselves, *What does that poor fellow's wife feed him*?

Although I couldn't see over these mountainous packages, somehow I navigated my way to the check-out counter. I pushed my cart into the cart lane and stepped into the customer line. I was delighted to see only one person in front of me.

Oh, no! It was my next-door neighbor.

She turned to me and smiled, "Nice day."

She then stared down at my cart and looked again at me. She knew that only Dana and I occupied our house. I was sure she was thinking, *What on G-D's earth do these people eat?*

She picked up her bags, looked at the cart and smirked at me, "Have a nice lunch!"

I drove back home and dropped off the package. I said to Dana, "If we hurry up, we can still make it to the beach and start our vacation."

It was our lucky day. No traffic. We were at the hotel in record time.

"Hey, let's rush off to the beach before we lose the day," Dana said.

Where to sit? Where to lay our stuff down? Location! Location! Location! This would be our new home.

"I don't want to sit in the crowded section," exclaimed Dana.

"Yes, but I've had a lot of coffee this morning. I need to sit near the facilities."

We compromised. We found a spot away from the most crowded area, but not too far from the rest rooms.

We both read for about an hour. Then, I had an urgent call to get up and go. Fortunately, I made it to the grubby rest room in time. I wiped the toilet seat off very carefully with their toilet paper. I wished they had Costco's macho kind. There was water everywhere, anyway. I hoped it was just water. I hurried out.

Now, finding my way back to my blanket and my wife wasn't easy. Everything looked the same. And if one of those, "Can I help you police???" spotted me sadly looking around, I was dead meat.

"Do you know what you are looking for, Sir," they would ask, *Sir* being code for geezer. "Oh your wife? Do you remember what she looked like? Could you describe her?"

I was fortunate that one of those *"do-gooders"* did not approach me. I managed to find my way back to Dana on my own.

I noticed a lot of smiles coming my way. Most of them were coming from women. I was very glad I had spent so much time swimming over the winter. These smiles were no doubt a result of my looking *buff* as the kids would say. This was especially true for a harmless looking codger.

As I pulled up to our chairs, I nudged Dana with my foot, "Hey," I said. "Your old man is looking pretty *buff,* right?" Dana looked up from her book and laughed, "Yes, *Mr. Buff,* you look beautiful, especially with those bathroom tissues hanging out from your bathing suit."

36

Still Perplexed After All These Years

PERPLEXED IS ONE of those words - you hear it and you know what it means. However, it's certainly not a word you want your cardiologist to use.

The only time I use the word is when I'm thinking about the opposite sex.

I've been married for more than forty years. I have two daughters and a seven-year-old granddaughter. I have two wives: Esther, my actual wife, and Dana, my imaginary wife. Dana appears in some of my stories and is solely responsible for everything she says or might say. I have nothing to do with it, nor does Esther.

Given the fact that I'm actually surrounded by women, one would think I'd be less perplexed by them. Not a chance! I spent my youth trying to grow up in Dorchester, Massachusetts. I went to an all-boys' school. Saying the last thing on my mind was girls would be a colossal lie. However, it didn't matter, since I was probably the last thing on their minds, at least, as far as I knew.

My life should have been centered around school and acquiring knowledge. It wasn't. All that mattered to me were the seasonal sports my friends and I played.

On fall weekends we played tackle football down at Franklin Field. We considered it safer to get tackled onto the hard, rocky ground than to try speaking to a girl.

In the spring it was stickball. We played in between the houses. We broke a few windows, but not many hearts.

After high school graduation, I became a counselor at an all-boys' camp. Early on I went into town to buy ice cream and soda. It was there that I met a girl who was a counselor at an all-girls' camp. We both had the same night off.

We decided to spend all of our nights off together. We'd canoe to an island that lay between the two camps. We never figured out what the mosquitoes ate when we didn't meet. The good news for me was that we were supposed to be attending the same college in the fall. She was officially my first girlfriend.

I read somewhere that a woman makes up her mind in seconds as to the future of the relationship and prays that you don't say something stupid. I don't remember what I said, but it must have been pretty stupid. When the summer was over, we met briefly. I don't remember what it was that I said, but I never saw her again.

The following summer I went to a co-ed camp. The owner's niece and myself enjoyed a glorious summer together, along with the mosquitoes. I think they were the same hungry mosquitoes from the islands.

Summer ended. I called her house. Her father answered. This time, I must have said something really stupid to him. She never called back!

Years later I moved to New York City. A new acquaintance invited me to her party where I met a girl who was visiting from the University of Michigan. She was planning to stay for two weeks. She said, "I can't wait to see your apartment." She spent the rest of the summer there.

There is no better place to have fun than NYC, especially when you have no money. I had no money. There were no mosquitoes. Oh, my, did we have fun!

Fall came and she went back to school. She begged me not to go out with any other woman EVER. She also asked me to wear long sleeve shirts since she thought my arms were very attractive.

For a while we had many warm phone conversations and then we didn't. Unlike either of my previous girlfriends, she went into great detail as to all the stupid things I had said. Our romance ended abruptly. I went out and bought two short sleeve shirts.

As I mentioned before, I have two daughters, a seven-year-old granddaughter, and two wives, Esther and Dana. I try very hard not to say anything too stupid.

However, I'm still very perplexed when it comes to women!

I'm praying my cardiologist isn't perplexed about me.

37

The Apology

FACEBOOK NOTIFIED ME I had a message from someone called Pat Shaw. I assumed it was someone inviting me to a storytelling event thousands of miles away. I get those invites all the time. I usually don't respond.

This one read "Are you the Robert Isenberg that I knew many years ago in NYC? I was Pat Steinberger then. I thought I found you once and sent you an email, to which you didn't respond. I suppose you won't now. If you are the Robert I knew, I'm sorry I acted so badly. I hope you are doing well. You look as though you are. You were a smart, funny, charismatic man then, so it's no surprise. I wish you well." It was signed "Pat".

I showed my wife, Dana, Pat's email. She laughed and said, "That's quite the list of compliments. Are you going to answer her? You probably should."

"I'm not sure. Why would anyone apologize for something they did years ago?" I asked.

"Maybe she wants you back or maybe she's in some sort of apologizing group and they may have an agenda," Dana said.

I thought I'd email Pat to say that it's impossible because I was never any of those things she said I was, and besides she left off tall, dark, and handsome.

I spoke to a few friends, explaining that I received an apology, something that just about no one ever gets these days. In this case, it is about forty-five years later. The question that they all asked is, "Will you respond?"

I thought I might. I could mention my website to her. One of my posted stories is called "I WAS A NERD BEFORE THERE WAS SUCH A WORD." There is a segment in that story about a Pat I once knew.

I met the actual Pat at a party in Manhattan in the early spring. She came home with me to my apartment on 85th street and didn't leave until fall. Pat had come to NYC from the University of Michigan. She was planning on spending the summer in Manhattan with the black convertible her daddy had given her for her 19th birthday. She had been living with her friend, Nancy, before me.

Pat cooked exotic Hungarian and French dishes while she lectured me on Bob Dylan's and Leonard Cohen's lyrics, explaining to me that their lyrics were much more than song lyrics. They were poetry. I said little, but ate a lot.

Pat fixed up my friend, Jake, with her friend, Nancy. It seemed as if the fix-up was going fine, but then Nancy confessed to me that she didn't like Jake much and didn't like Pat at all.

Nancy then asked me to sleep with her. I said that I didn't think it would be too good an idea. She called me a loser and told me to grow up. I thought it was well-meaning advice. I made a mental note to work on it. I should have written it down.

When summer ended, Pat went back to the University of Michigan shedding many tears. She asked me not to date anyone else for the rest of my life.

Soon our phone conversations grew heavy, difficult and distant. Finally, Pat ranted that I was needy, dependent and vapid. She also mentioned that her roommate, whom I had never met, totally agreed with her. I thought they both had a point, especially the dependent part. I wasn't too sure about needy, but I thought vapid had kind of a ring to it.

Before Pat hung up for the last time, she exclaimed that she had never had an orgasm with me and that she had faked them all.

I said I had never had one either and had faked mine as well.

But I got the last word. Here she is, forty-five years later, apologizing to me, and I still haven't responded to her email.

38

Retirement Is Not to Be Taken Lightly

I'VE HAD A lot of jobs in my life. I've counted cars in downtown Boston during a blizzard. I've tried to sell encyclopedias after school. I've been a waiter. I've been a bartender. I've even been a cook. I've worked for people I didn't like. I've worked for people who didn't like me.

I started a business when I was in my early twenties called *Robert's Fairly Famous Roast Beef Sandwiches*. It serviced three single bars in downtown Manhattan. It had its moments. Since there was a hamburger chain called Prexy's, which claimed their burgers had a *college education*, I said not only are our sandwiches *illiterate but they're thick*

Not too long ago, my wife, Dana, and I sold our business called *Right Stuff, Inc. Right Stuff* had two offices. One in Shanghai and one in Burlington, Mass. We serviced companies like Walmart, Stride Rite, and Carter's. None of these jobs or businesses were easy. They all came with issues.

But none of these "issues" came even close to the issue of retirement. Retirement is a full-time job and then some. Retirement requires focus just as the previous jobs did. The problem is, I find it impossible to focus. I'm never sure if I should be reading the *Wall Street Journal* or folding my socks. Both take total concentration. The *Wall Street Journal* is jam-packed with valuable information. It even has amusing little essays regarding everything you never thought of before you read the essay. It reviews movies, books, plays and other things you never thought of. Why then does it put me to sleep?

Socks are a whole other issue. They really don't come out of the dryer matching. When they went in, they matched. However in my retirement, I've come up with a cure for non-matching socks. Who cares? Nobody will see them anyway. They are safely hidden under your pants.

I know that it's important to stay busy. I've read article after article about the importance of that. Keeping busy keeps the mind fertile. "Fertile?" That might explain the unwanted growths on my scalp.

These never-ending retirement advisers also say, "Take the time to do tasks that you have put off for years."

That's an easy one for me. It's clutter! I know I'll get to those magazines that have been piling up for years. I address one pile. The first magazine I pick up is a Vanity

Fair. The cover has a picture of Charlize Theron in a bikini. It also headlines an article called "The Friction Between Clinton and Gore." I check the date; December 2000. That's not so long ago. It goes back in the pile.

I thumb through a New Yorker dated January 16, 2012. *That's practically yesterday,* I muse. It also gets dropped back in the pile.

I then decide to go through my clothes. I go in my closet and take out a suit I designed in Taiwan. I think, *That's a long time ago.* I put it on. It fits. I show Dana and say, "I'm going to give away some clothes."

Dana looks at the suit. "Perfect," she says. "Not that one."

I've retired, but not totally. I work on my stories for writers group and two newspapers every week. There is very bad chemistry between my computer and me. My computer has attitude! I realize the computer is far more intelligent than I am. It can spell better. It remembers the rules of grammar better than I do.

What I can't forgive is its arrogance. When I misspell a word and go to spellcheck, the computer responds, *"Perhaps, if you got closer to the correct spelling of the word, I could help you."*

Yesterday, when I left my article on the computer to stop for a bite, my computer changed an entire paragraph. What's worse, it left a note, *"If you are attending writers group this week, they will be surprised and pleased with how smoothly this paragraph flows now."*

Then there is the computer language. It includes words that used to have meaning to me, such as *Server! File! Desktop! Folder! Cloud!* Before I retired I knew what those words meant. They were actual physical entities!

Recently I asked Dana if she had noticed that people who used to speak clearly were mumbling. Dana asked, "Did you ever notice the hearing aid office downtown?"

My response was, "What?"

We went downtown to the office together. My first reaction was that the aids were too small. Elderly people will misplace them and then not be able to see them. The batteries were teeny-weeny. All I could think was that they could be mistaken for pills. If I swallowed them, I could hear Dana saying, "I always told you to listen to your inner voice."

Retirement is not to be taken lightly, and I'm just getting started.

V

Travel

39

Security and Insecurity

IT WAS ALL perfect! What could be better! I had made a reservation for my wife, Dana, and I at Punta Cana. I also booked a reservation for my daughter, Rebecca, and her husband, Joshua, at the same hotel. I booked us on an early flight leaving Boston at 5:58 A.M.

"For what time should I set the alarm?" asked Dana. "The plane leaves at 5:58 A.M. We want to be there at least an hour before flight time. How do they come up with 5:58? Can't they round it off to 6:00 A.M?"

"Why don't you give them a call?" I ask.

"I just might do that. Anyway, I need an answer. What time do you want to get up? I need to set the alarm," Dana said.

"I guess 2:45. We'll need at least an hour to get out the door. We'll finish packing the car in the morning. We should leave here no later than 4:15. That should get us to the parking lot by 4:45 and to the airport by 5:00."

The next morning, the alarm went off at 2:45. Dana nudged me, "It's quarter to three."

I rolled over, "So?"

"So get up!" yelled Dana.

"I need ten more minutes."

Dana nudged me again at 3:05. "Get up! I don't want to miss our flight. Get up, now!"

I stumbled out of bed, found my shaving razor and then tried to find my face. What ordinarily takes three or four minutes took a lot longer. I didn't do much better with brushing my teeth. I then took an awakening shower. I should have reversed the order and showered first. By the time I was fully dressed and had added six or seven questionable objects to my suitcase, it was 4:29.

"We are going to miss the flight," Dana exclaimed.

"Excuse me. Did you forget that you are traveling with the Business Travel Pro?"

We made good time to the offsite parking lot. We parked where the woman told us. We waited only a minute or two for the shuttle bus. We climbed on board. It was 5:02. We were in good time. We figured the shuttle would have very few people going to the airport at that hour. Wrong! Five couples arrived, all fumbling with their luggage. We were finally ready to leave for the airport when the driver got a call. She was told she had to stay and wait for one more passenger.

"We're dead in the water," Dana sighed.

"You keep forgetting with whom you are traveling!"

We finally got to the airport and presented ourselves to the woman who took our bags and did whatever they do with the tickets to give us our boarding passes. Dana was worried about having enough time to get through security and be at the gate before the plane took off.

The woman waved us off. "You'll be fine," she said before resuming her conversation with her fellow workers. We scrambled off to security.

"Finally," I thought, "There You Go Business Pro" just like the ad says. I had my slip-on shoes. No laces. There would be no fumbling. I would show all these people that this one old guy knew a thing or two about security. I placed all my items neatly in the tray, except my computer, which I properly placed in its own tray. We approached the security apparatus.

I was about to walk in and set my feet in the markers when the security lady said, "Remove your belt, sir!"

"My belt? Why? It's made of cotton."

"Sir, remove your belt!"

"I've had this belt forever. It's never caused any trouble that I know about. I promise to keep my eye on it and make sure it doesn't cause a problem."

"Sir, remove your belt and place it in the small white tray now!"

I began to take the belt off. Naturally, it got hung up in every pant loop. I turned to look at the passengers behind me. They did not look pleased. I could see they were thinking that because of this old buzzard, we're not going to have time for coffee, or worse, we'll miss our flight.

Finally, I got the belt off and went through security. As I was picking up my items, Dana said, "You don't have time to put your belt back on Mr. Travel Pro. Our gate is the last one."

There I was holding my computer bag over one shoulder and keeping my pants up with my other hand. "There you go Business Pro," I whimpered to myself.

I hobbled to the gate and handed my boarding pass to the woman gate keeper. She took a long look at me holding up my pants and shook her head. She didn't say a word. She didn't have to.

Next time we had an early flight, I'd get up when Dana told me to so I wouldn't end up clutching at my beltless pants and praying I wasn't going to make more of an exhibition of myself than I already had.

40

The Red Jacket

A TRIP TO Vegas and, of course, there had to be a story. Vegas is a microcosm of the United States. Could you use the word ostentatious to describe Vegas? Not really. Would grandiose work? It doesn't do Vegas justice. No, the only description for Vegas is the phrase "not enough". There is no such thing as "enough" in Vegas.

So, I thought, perhaps, I should tell of the people who sit down in front of the slots - the ones who are afraid to break for lunch because someone else might come to get their winnings after all their hard work of pulling the slot's arm. Should I tell of the shows that I rarely go to see because I get done working way too late? Should I tell of the long hours of sitting up and waiting, waiting for the purchasing agents to keep their appointments? I don't think so. Should I tell of the amazing indoor restaurants under the incredible clouds as I look above at the never-changing blue sky?

The hostesses actually ask if we want inside or outside. The gondoliers are bursting out with their "O Solo O Mio" renditions. Street merchants are hawking gelato. Can this really be happening? Is it all too surreal? Shall I tell this all to you in detail? I choose not to.

Rather, I choose to tell of my ten-year-old red Land's End jacket, which I left on the plane that had carried me and my jacket from Boston to Vegas. It wasn't until I arrived at the Venetian Hotel that I realized that I had left my jacket on the flight. How did I come to this realization? What caught my attention? Certainly, I didn't need my jacket in Vegas. It was 77 degrees outside and 69 degrees in the room. It was what was in my pockets that caught my attention: certainly not the winter gloves, not the package of gum, not the breath mints; nope, not the car keys. Those I would worry about on Monday when I returned to Logan Airport. Medication? I could make it three days without it. But how could I get along without my trusted hair brush?

As I came out of the bathroom, I checked the mirror. *Another bad hair day.* Where was my hair brush? Uh oh! *Where did I put my jacket?* Yes, then it came to me. I had placed my jacket in the bulkhead in front of my seat because there hadn't been enough room in my overhead compartment. What to do? Whom to call? I began with America West's 800 number: a joke! The only responses were worthless recorded messages. Nothing could stop me now. I put on my Sherlock Holmes hat and somehow found a local number for America West. After at least four calls that took me on a circuitous route, I scored. I actually discovered the local Lost and Found number.

I called at about twelve o'clock noon and listened to a message explaining that somebody was always on duty between the hours of 9:00 A.M. and 2:00 P.M. I left a message that I had left my red Land's End jacket with critical medication and car keys in the pocket. I didn't mention my hair brush. This was on Thursday. I included my name, hotel number, and room number. No call back on Thursday. I called three times on Friday between the hours of 9:00 A.M. and 2:00 P.M. only to reach the same message. Saturday was a repeat of Friday, except that I tried calling four times and my wife tried once. On Sunday, when Dana drove our daughter to the airport, she went to various locations at America West. Finally, she was told that if my jacket had been found it would be sent to Phoenix, America West's home for wayward jackets.

A friend from Boston called to tell me about Sunday's brutal Nor'easter that would most likely be greeting my planned arrival. He asked me if I was worried about getting home. I told him of my red jacket plight, the missing medication, and the car keys. I did not mention the hair brush, but said that the only thing that will worry me is that when I board the plane, the pilot will be wearing my red jacket. At 4:30 P.M. on Sunday, as we were checking out, my phone rang. It was Frank from America West. They had found my red jacket. I could pick it up at the airport. He carefully briefed me that when I arrived at the airport, I was to report to "Special Situations" and explain that Frank had called me and that my jacket would be in the Auditing department. When I introduced myself to the "Special Situations" person, I explained to him that Frank had called at about 4:30 P.M. to tell me that my red jacket would be safely placed in the auditing room. He told me that all missing articles are sent to Phoenix and that mine would be no exception. Also, he had never heard of anybody named Frank. He explained that Lost and Found people were only on duty from 9:00 A.M. to 2 P.M., so how could this Frank possibly have called at 4:30 P.M.?

Finally, he relented and said he would look if I gave him my ID—in this case my license. At this point, I would have given him my entire wallet.

He went behind the door and after about ten minutes came back out and asked, "What color did you say it was?"

I told him my jacket was red and the pockets contained my car keys and my medication. I didn't mention my hair brush.

He went back again. My heart was beating. What seemed like forever was probably another 7 to 8 minutes. He appeared with my red jacket.

A round-trip ticket from Boston to Vegas: $275.00. A hotel room at the Venetian: $300.00. A bet on the Kansas City Chiefs to win the 2007 Super bowl: $10.00.

A ten-year-old Land's End jacket costing $80.00 containing my hair brush: priceless!

41

Face It

I'VE LIVED WITH my face a lot longer than I ever expected to. In fact, my face and I have been around for quite some time. I've learned a few things; not nearly as much as I would like to have, but then who has?

Let's, however, get back to my face. For better or worse, I have no idea - no idea, whatsoever - what people see in my face.

There was a time when people looked at me and simply had to tell me how much money they had. Very often, it would come from persons I had never met before.

Once while I was waiting to board a flight in Japan's Narita airport, the poorly dressed man standing directly in front of me suddenly turned around and said, "Don't let my clothes fool you. A few years ago, I received a stock tip. I made a bloody fortune on it!"

I replied that I was very happy to hear that, and since we'd be on the same flight, I wished him a very safe flight.

I was putting my clothes on at the tennis club's locker room when the man at the next locker, whose name I still don't know, was taking his jacket from the locker.

He closed the locker door and turned to look at me, "I was a pharmacist before I retired. Before I quit working, I bought a piece of land for thirty-five thousand dollars."

He continued, "I sold it last week for eight million."

He put his locker key in his pocket and hurried off without saying goodbye.

Dana and I were leaving a movie I had despised. As we were about to leave the theatre, I said to Dana, "God, that movie was awful!"

Dana retorted, "You probably missed half of it. You were snoring. I loved the movie."

The very attractive woman in front of us turned and smiled at me, "I agree with your wife."

Her husband gave us a friendly look and said, "Let's go over to Bertucci's across the street and discuss the movie."

We ordered four glasses of the house red and before anything was said about the movie, the husband offered that they lived in Andover. He boasted that they had no kids and as a result, they had socked away a lot of dough.

The wife seemed somewhat embarrassed and wanted to know if we had kids.

"Two girls," I said.

He looked at us sadly, probably imagining that we were spending whatever monies we had on our two girls. He grabbed the bill, paid it and then motioned for his wife to get up and leave with him. They did.

My face doesn't just inspire money talk. It has inspired many other unsolicited comments.

I was waiting for my car in a New York City garage alongside an elderly woman. She was staring at me and finally, with a heavy accent, she said, "I saw you on TV last night. You were wonderful! Funny! So funny I couldn't stop laughing."

"Do you remember my name?" I asked.

"No," she smiled, "but I can't wait to watch you again."

I was gathering my bags at LAX. A man and his son approached me. The father looked at me very seriously, "I'd like your autograph for my son here."

"What name should I put down?" I murmured.

"I figured you for a wise guy," he growled. "I saw your last movie and you stunk!!"

With that comment and muttering something about my lineage, he stalked away.

42

Summer Is Over, But Not My Questions

I THOUGHT BRIEFLY about naming this piece "Gnats to the Gnats." I reconsidered because I have many questions about summer and they don't stop with gnats.

My question regarding gnats is *what do gnats really want*? In my case, they mostly live at the top of my front walk. They wait patiently there for me to come and pick up the newspapers. One or two will light upon me as I walk to the front. I can almost hear them saying, "*He's old and can't move quickly. Let's swarm him!! Let's get to his ears and eyes.*" They don't bite or sting. They just circle around me like an evil cloud.

So, what's up with them? Perhaps, we misjudge them and all they want is to be friends. They just are not exactly sure how to go about it.

I googled gnats. There were countless articles on how to get rid of them. One suggested a pan of vinegar and soap. No doubt the gnats would assume it was salad dressing and get stuck on the soap. There were a few lines describing them as small, non-biting, harmless insects.

Now how would we humans feel if we were googled and it said we were basically harmless and for the most part didn't bite, but that we needed to be exterminated?

I have all winter to think it over. Maybe gnats need a second chance.

My next question is who taught seagulls to read. When googling seagulls, one will find *Nine Fascinating Facts You May Not Know About Seagulls*. They are right. I did not know any of them. However, what was not mentioned is that seagulls were somehow taught to read and in English. I've got proof.

Have I mentioned that I go to Ogunquit every summer? Every summer, I hear horrific tales of aggressive seagulls stealing lunches. I hear how they open metal lunch boxes with their beaks and tear apart lobster shells without nutcrackers. But how does one explain that the restaurant on the beach that serves very delicious everything has never seen a seagull even approach their wide-open windows? Why?

There is a sign at the top of the restaurant next to the clock. It reads:

TOPS REQUIRED! NO BARE FEET!
NO WET BATHING SUITS!

NO DOGS!
NO SEAGULLS!

So, there you have your proof that seagulls can read and obey.

My last observation and question regarding summer is the question everyone asks after Labor Day, "Where did the summer go?"

What do people want from summer? It has the same amount of days as all the other seasons. No more, no less. But every Labor Day party, you hear people moaning, "What happened to my summer? I hardly got any vacation time. The last thing I remember is Memorial Day! And then whoosh!"

Think of the bright side: No more mosquitoes. No more BBQ's with all those delicious-but-horrible-for-you hot dogs that you can't stop eating. No more beach traffic that simply doesn't move or lunch-snatching, lobster-cracking, too-smart-for-their-own-good seagulls. No more lawn that needs mowing every other day. Even those vacations you didn't get to take meant packing and unpacking.

More importantly, no more worrying about what those social-climbing gnats want!

Next time you ask, "Where did summer go?" Just think, "*Thank G-D it's over!*"

43

Pool Savvy in Shanghai

I PLACE MY water toys carefully by the end of the pool. I need them to be within easy reach. Once again, I slide into the warmth of this magnificent pool. Certainly, it's within reason that I stay at this hotel. To me, most hotels provide the same essentials - a bed, a shower, a TV, and a phone. I rarely eat in a hotel, if ever. None of the Shanghai hotels provide real heat and I've been to some of the best. But I would never try another hotel in Shanghai no matter what. I love their pool. It's probably about 84 degrees F, but there is no one here who could verify that as a fact. The staff is more than polite. They greet me with genuine warmth and say, "You are back to swim again."

I smile and say, "Yes, yes I am." They smile again.

I begin my routine of about twenty minutes, using one style, an exercise taught to me by Igor Burdenko, a water therapist. I move my arms and my legs and my head clears almost immediately. As usual, the pool is empty. The only sound I hear is my body rippling through the water. One staff member watches me through the glass partition. He is fully clothed. I suppose he is there in case I drown so he can call housekeeping to clean up the mess.

I think I can do this forever, but it's 10:10 P.M., and they close at exactly 11:00 P.M. I look up to see a man and woman place their towels on a chaise lounge and then slip into the pool. He is probably mid-fifties. She is maybe twenty-five. These are my favorite ages for a couple. If only he had been mid-sixties like me, I would have been even more pleased. She is laughing at everything he says. They are locked together as one as they try to swim.

He looks at me and asks me where I come from. This is extremely unusual. Most other swimmers avert their eyes as if I were not there, never mind seeking a conversation. I learned to do the same. Most pool intruders are Western. Both of them are Asian.

I answer, "The States. Boston. Where are you from?"

"I'm from San Diego and she is from Beijing," he says.

"Oh, nice," I say and stupidly ask, "What brings you here?"

"Business," he responds and then adds, "I come here every month."

I am thinking "Why so infrequently?" as I look again at her. He goes back to talking to her and she throws her head back laughing.

After a few more minutes, they climb out and share one chaise lounge; the chaise he had placed his towel on. I will not look. I cannot look. I don't have to look. I have my pool back and all is safe in my world.

I reach up to gather one of my swim toys when *she* strides in. Oh, my goodness. I look at her. Lord have mercy. She is the "dream" Asian woman. Even the laughing girl on the chaise lounge takes her in and, for a minute or two, stops laughing.

Gracefully, she enters the pool. She never notices that I am there or if she does, she doesn't care. She does laps and I do my Burdenko thing around the perimeter of the pool. Our radar keeps us far apart. She swims one more lap and pulls herself up the ladder and stretches out on another chaise lounge. I will not look! I cannot look! I don't have to look! She closes her eyes. I continue to circle the pool. Soon the pool will close and I will return to my room, perhaps to watch another Steven Segal movie.

Did I hear correctly? She is asking me why I swim for so long. Should I answer that I'm trying to build back arteries so that my heart will get all of the oxygen it needs so that I might live longer. I think not. I'm pretty certain that discussions about hearts and arteries do not make for fluid conversation, especially with a young person.

I look up at her perfect face, her perfect body, and her perfect skin.

"What else could I be doing?" I ask.

She ignores my question and asks "Where are you from?"

I tell her that I am from the States.

"Where are you from?" I ask.

"Beijing," she answers.

The laughing girl looks over and then smiles as her lover whispers something in her ear.

"What brings you to Shanghai?" I ask.

"My uncle manages this hotel. I come here to rest."

"What do you do in Beijing?" I ask.

"I'm a graduate student in the university," she says. "Do you like this hotel?" she asks, changing the subject.

Before I can reply, she says, "This hotel has an aroma."

"I never have smelled anything peculiar," I reply.

She says, "I said this hotel is older." She seems to realize my hearing mistake and she says "I didn't say aroma; I said older."

My only excuse is Chinese people have a problem with their L's, so older could sound like aroma.

"Yes, it's older, but well kept," I say, hoping she picks up the praise for her uncle.

She smiles and asks if I like China.

"Very much," I reply.

I can see from her smile that I have finally given the correct answer.

"Do you come often?" she asks.

"Twice a year, every November and every May," I tell her. She asks, "Have you been to Beijing?"

"Not yet," I reply.

"Oh, you must come to Beijing. You can't come to China without visiting Beijing," she informs me.

"I'm sure you will be my guide when I come," I tell her.

"Of course," she says, both of us knowing that it is more likely that my car will fly me to Beijing.

The pool attendant, who has not moved from the other side of the partition, comes through and points to the clock. It reads 10:55.

She rises from the chaise lounge. I try my best not to gape at her. She looks down as I am paddling towards the pool stairs.

"Nice to meet you. See you tomorrow," she says.

"Yes," I say, thinking about another Steven Segal movie and some Chinese cookies. Would I or could I ask for anything more?

44

This Land Is Your Land,
This Land Is My Land

AS WE DROVE off to Maine from our Lexington home, I said to my wife, Dana, "Do you ever think we are being watched?"

"No," Dana replied. "I won't ask why, since I'm very sure you will tell me."

"Well, we always leave this Subaru at the top of the driveway in front of our house, right? Now, if I were even a semi-smart robber who was watching our house and us, I would think open season on the Isenberg home."

"Funny," Dana said. "I was thinking how much I'm looking forward to this trip. You know how much I love being near the ocean. You know how much I'm looking forward to walking on the beach at low tide. You know how much I am looking forward to the breakfast at the Terrace, reading the Times and gazing at the surf. No, I wasn't thinking about robbers who might be watching. I was actually feeling pretty good about leaving the house. I checked to make sure all the lights were out and all the doors locked. Yes, I was feeling good. I know that you showed Jeff where all the plants were, especially the ones out of sight. Will Jeff water every day?"

"Jeff sent me his teaching schedule. Yes, he will be teaching tennis every day. He promised me that he would water every day. He also promised to email me as to how the plants were doing," I said.

"That's good," said Dana. "One less thing you have to worry about."

We arrived at the Terrace by The Sea in a little over an hour. We congratulated ourselves for leaving on a no-traffic Thursday. We were on the beach and in the water until there was no sun left. It was all perfect.

Dana and I played catch with what looked like a part football and part plastic, feather-shaped thing. A young couple that was watching us finally came over. It seemed they couldn't praise us enough. The guy was saying how impressed he was at our throwing and catching agility.

When they left, Dana laughed, "I think they were impressed that at our age we were still moving. I don't think they were really complimenting us on our athletic ability."

I once again carried my tattered boogie board out to meet the highest and most ferocious wave that would carry me to the shore and Dana's clapping. It was clear by the astonished glances that if I weren't the oldest boogie boarder in the universe, I was in the running.

Then there were the long walks on the endless sand. It was hard to tell what was more glorious—the sun on our backs as we walked to the footbridge or the gentle breeze in our face as we returned to our chairs.

I had brought at least a dozen New Yorker magazines. This would be my chance to try and catch up. My goal was to read at least two stories each day and try not to get caught up in one of their endless narratives. Dana was more than content with her Kindle.

The evenings were spent deciding to which restaurant to go. We usually ended up in one of the more romantic outdoor restaurants, eating one kind of fish or another.

Dana has a habit of multi-listening. She barely listens to what I'm saying, but I can tell by the way her eyes sparkle that she is listening intently to the neighboring table's conversation. Usually, she keeps her eyes on me so as not to get caught. However, this time, she grabbed my hand and whispered, "While the woman was on her cell, the guy thought he'd try to steal one of her barbeque ribs. He only got his hand slapped."

As soon as the woman put away her cell phone, Dana became engrossed in conversation with the woman. There were some connections and exchanging of cards that would most likely never be looked at again.

After a walk downtown to the bakery, we would return to our cottage. I would check the email each night, and each night, there was a note from Jeff elaborating how well he was doing watering all the plants and how they were flourishing under his care.

That is until the night before we left. Jeff's email said, "I have good news and bad news. Your cherry tomatoes that are hanging from the deck are safe, but your other vegetables have been decimated by what I suspect is a groundhog. When I arrived in your backyard, I found a half-eaten cucumber and all the cucumber leaves gone. The peppers, basil, and dill are all gone as well."

I read Jeff's email very slowly to Dana, "I told you we were being watched. I just didn't think we were being watched by a groundhog."

I don't know if I've seen too many Disney movies or my imagination has gotten the better of me, but when we returned home, there was the groundhog with a stick in his hand leading the chipmunks, rabbits and squirrels to a chorus of Woodie Guthrie's *This Land is Your Land, This Land is My Land.*

45

Do I Look like Somebody Who Knows How to Put Up a Tent

STEP 1: INSERT one of the main tent poles from rear side through the two sleeve sections on the left side to point B.

Step 2: Repeat the above step but with two sleeves on the right side.

From point ref G-H.

There were nine more steps to putting up this "EASY UP TENT."

My career took me to many places in both the United States and some of the rest of the world. I thought because I had to work so hard, I always deserved at least one day at the beach. As a result, I have enjoyed many beaches throughout the world.

I have swum, surfed, boogie-boarded and just plain ogled at many beaches. My theory was that mostly my eyes needed refreshing. I never found a beach that wasn't easy on my eyes.

It had always been my way to show up at these beaches with only my bathing suit and a good-sized towel.

A few years ago, my wife, Dana, decided that we needed beach chairs. Her reasoning was that lying on the sand was not good for our backs. Beach chairs come not only in assorted colors but with assorted mechanics. Trying to open one of these chairs in public can be most embarrassing. Some open from the top; some the bottom. The embarrassment frequently came when a new-found beach neighbor noted my struggles.

Usually, they would begin with, "May I help you, Sir?"

Bad enough they felt the need to offer to help, they had to add the *Sir – as I said before* being code for geezer.

This year, Dana mentioned that we had to purchase a tent.

"A tent!" I exclaimed. "Why?"

Dana explained, "I just heard from Sarah. She and our granddaughter, Finleigh, are going to join us in Ogunquit, Maine. I'm sure you know how sensitive a five-year-old's skin can be. Finleigh is no exception."

"Who is going to put up this tent?" I inquired.

"What we'll do is practice putting it up in private. When we get it right we'll bring it to the beach," Dana explained

"You know, although I don't think I ever mentioned it, when I was in the army, they had a thing they called bivouac. Sounds like maybe it could be a French delicacy.

It wasn't! It was the army's version of camping.

There was always someone yelling something like, *Hey, eight-ball, where did you learn to put up an eight-ball tent?* My tent was always coming unconstructed. How the gods knew we were bivouacking, I don't know, but they did because they always sent a cold, very damp rain and a stiff breeze. You can guess the results. *Hey, eight-ball, you better put it back up quick or you'll drown.* As you might guess, I don't have fond memories of tents."

Dana was insistent, "Finleigh and Sarah are both asking for a tent. We'll be fine. Like I said, we'll practice back at the cabin. We'll get the hang of it. Pardon the pun."

We picked Sarah and Finleigh up at Logan Airport and traveled back to the beach. We'd only had time to practice putting up the tent once. It had not been successful.

Their first day at the beach, we placed our chairs, two boogie boards and a multitude of sundry items on our beach cart. We had bought the beach cart a year ago. Although beach carts can present some harrowing moments, fortunately, we had a year of experience. As a result, our daughter was impressed by our cart know-how.

Thankfully, neither Finleigh nor Sarah asked for the tent on their first day.

The following day, our friends, Jeff and Karen, were coming up.

Jeff is not only an engineer; he's also a professor at MIT. Upon their arrival, even before we ate or even exchanged niceties, I handed Jeff the directions to putting up the tent.

Jeff read them cautiously and carefully. "Well, Jeff, what do you think?" I asked.

"If you don't try to help, I'll get it up in five minutes." How did he know?

Jeff went to work on the tent. The rest of us stood around admiring his tent expertise. I didn't try to help. I stayed busy scratching my head a lot as I watched in silence. The tent did go up, though it took Jeff a lot longer than five minutes, but who was counting? Probably, only me.

Jeff and Karen left the next day. Sarah offered to put up the tent.

I said I'd help.

Sarah said, "I'd rather do it myself, Dad."

What? I felt like asking her, *Do I look like somebody who doesn't know how to put up a tent?*

46

Scenes from a Winter Haven

I ONLY SEE three of you. I'll give you one minute to find the other two or I'm giving your table away!"

"I'll take it!" shouted a voice from off on the side.

This was a hamburger place on a Wednesday night about five o'clock. There were about twenty people milling around waiting for their name to be called.

We had found out that if there weren't at least a forty-minute wait even with a reservation, we were at the wrong restaurant. This feeding frenzy begins at about four o'clock and simmers down around eight.

Welcome to Delray Beach, Florida. We arrived on a Tuesday evening. My wife, Dana, promptly called a restaurant we had heard about. The hostess asked Dana when could we be there? Dana told her in about twenty minutes.

"Perfect!" the hostess said. "We'll have a table waiting for you."

Fifteen minutes later, we were there! We tried to get the hostess's attention so she'd know we'd arrived. There were at least seven people circling around the beleaguered woman. Finally, there was a brief clearing. I told her my name and what had been promised. She didn't reply.

I asked, "Doesn't a reservation mean anything here?" This time, the hostess responded, "It means something." She turned and walked away.

I looked at Dana. "Do you have any idea what 'something' means?"

Dana laughed. "I thought I knew what 'something' meant. Maybe not."

"What do you want to do?" I asked Dana.

"Let's see how this plays out," Dana said.

We walked over to where many other people were waiting. "What time was your reservation for?" a woman asked.

Before I could answer, she said, "Don't even think about it. They'll get to you when they get to you. Are you two married?"

"Yes," I answered.

"Is this your second marriage?"

"No, we've been married for a long time."

"So, any grandchildren?"

"Yes, we have a five-year-old granddaughter.

"Most people down here have a lot more."

"Oh," I said. "Good information. We'll try to do better."

Dana addressed the group, "Do any of you know what it means when the hostess says your reservation means 'something'?"

The husband of the woman who had been asking me questions shook his head as if he were talking to two idiots, "Yeah, it means sit down and shut up."

Their party was called to their table. They wished us good luck.

We finally were seated about fifty minutes after our promised time. We knew we must be in a pretty decent restaurant. Also, everyone seems to talk to everyone in Delray, whether they know them or not.

The next morning at breakfast, Dana was on her cell phone. An elderly gentleman walked over to our table. He nudged Dana with his cane.

"What are you doing on your phone? Your husband is sitting across from you. What's so important? What, are you talking to the president?"

Dana looked at him, "As a matter of fact, I am."

"What does he want?" asked the man.

"Money!" said Dana.

"Are you giving him any?"

"Not anymore! It all goes for political TV ads. We think they are as bad for us as cigarette ads were," Dana said as she stared back at him.

He shook his head and walked away.

That evening, we decided to check out the local Whole Foods. Getting anywhere is interesting. The speed limit on the highways is seventy. A joke! We were doing eighty. We were passed on both sides as if we were standing still.

The cars passing us were doing about eighty-five or ninety and they were getting passed! At various points,

I spotted State Troopers in waiting. I wondered what was considered excess speed. I saw no one pulled over.

We found a Whole Foods in a strip mall. There seem to be more strip malls in Delray than there are in all of New England. But no matter how many strip malls there are, parking is always at a premium. We found a spot. I pulled in on a slight angle to give us extra room to open our doors.

There was a woman sitting in the car next to my side. She had one arm hanging out the window and the other hand holding her cell phone.

"You parked crooked," she shouted. "When you open your door, don't hit my car! Where did you learn to drive?"

"Boston," I replied.

"Figures!" she exclaimed.

Dana mused. "What's up with her?"

"I think she may be on an undercover assignment. I believe it's her job to tell us Northerners how to park."

After shopping, we came back to our car. She was still sitting in her car. I opened my car door. I glanced at her. She was shaking her head at us. We had been in Florida only two days. She was the third person to shake their head at us.

Evidently, we had a lot to learn about getting along in Florida.

47

Delray Beach and Lexington, Mass Have Their Differences!

"*GRANDPA! GRANDPA!!*"
Twelve heads turned. Whether I wish to admit it or not, I'm in the land of the elderly. Delray is not that far from Lexington, Massachusetts. Well, maybe twelve hundred miles, but it's like another country.

I could start with the weather, but why bother. Almost everybody knows what goes on here in the Northeast in winter, and almost everybody knows that the inhabitants of Delray Beach, Florida, say it's cold when it's sixty-five degrees.

I've spent eight weeks in Delray Beach, where my wife Dana's Mom had been living for the past two winters and discovered Delray Beach has attitude.

I recall what happened with our last year's reservation at a popular restaurant.

"The table will be waiting for you," Dana was told.

It wasn't. The hostess was unreachable since she was surrounded by at least fifteen other equally irate customers.

Another "something" that happens daily is that the restaurants in the general area of Dana's Mom's place fill up to the brim by four-thirty and by seven-thirty, you could roll three bowling balls down any one of them without any danger of striking anybody.

However, downtown, it's the complete opposite. It seems that if you are over twenty-five, you need a permit to cross into the downtown area. Nothing and I mean *Nothing* happens in the downtown restaurants until seven-thirty and then SLAM-BAM-ALACAZAM, they are all jammed. It's like two separate cities molded into one.

It's not just the restaurants. The driving is more than interesting. Perhaps, the bumper sticker that says, "WHEN I GET OLD I'LL GO NORTH AND DRIVE SLOW!" suggests the horror of getting behind a driver in the passing lane going ten miles per hour and also making uncalled for frequent stops. In opposition are the drivers driving at NASCAR speeds and cutting in and out.

I'm not sure which of the two followed me into a strip mall, but one did. The driver decided to not just blow the horn at me, but to hold it down for at least two minutes. The reason was that I had momentarily stopped at the strip's intersection. Now had I realized that that person was in a huge hurry to get to Home Depot, I certainly would not have stopped at any silly old intersection. After all what was more important: getting home in one piece, or arriving at Home Depot three minutes earlier than planned?

On the first evening of our arrival, we were told there would be a block party. We were anxious to attend and meet our neighbors.

The gentleman sitting across from me asked what I thought of the State-Of-The-Union Address President Obama had delivered. I started to say that I was impressed, except I never got out the "ed" in impressed. The gentleman on my left began shouting, "He's done nothing!! Nothing!!!!" I thought *then why are they trying to repeal everything thing he's managed to accomplish?* I decided to say nothing.

We decided it would be important to attend the election for officers for Dana's mother's community. Coming from Lexington, we assumed the meeting would be quite civilized and mostly polite. It wasn't!!

There was much back and forth about what had been done about mulch and what hadn't been done. Turned out not much. Then the subject of driveways came up. One of the challengers asked the secretary, whose job he was seeking just how many driveways he had inspected.

The current secretary proudly said, "All three hundred and four."

"Well, you did a lousy job!!" shouted the challenger. That was Delray's version of polite talk.

Once again I leave Delray Beach, promising myself that next year I'll bring matching attitude with me.

48

Hey Ma, They're Trying to Kill Me!

I'M BACK IN Delray, Florida. I'm doing my best to eat properly. It's not easy. I've spent most of my life trying to be *food good*. Now as I age, it's even more important. Delray is not a very easy place to be food healthy. I promised myself to stay out of the delis.

These delis down here are lethal. They are easily as good as the ones that occupied Seventh Avenue in New York City. However, the other day, I had a few hungry guests.

"Would anyone like soup," I asked?

"Love some," was the response.

Okay, I thought it shouldn't be a problem going to the deli to pick up some chicken soup, and maybe cabbage soup. It was! I had to wait in a long line and watch these humongous corned beef sandwiches go by. Why hadn't I remembered?

It was just last year. I had visited this same deli at around eleven A.M. I ordered poached eggs and dry whole wheat toast. At the next table, a couple, at least ninety-five years old, were smacking down two huge pastrami sandwiches. I thought *what have they got to lose?* Probably, they thought the same. There I was with my runny poached eggs, feeling incredibly jealous of this ninety-five-year old couple. I paid for the soup and fled.

Our guests were from Boston and wanted to see the Patriot's football game. Anyone who watches football knows that there is maybe some football, but mostly ads. Who are the major sponsors? Subway, KFC, Pizza Hut, Little Caesar, to name a few. Did I ever in my life see more tantalizing pizzas than the ones they are displaying on my TV screen?

How about that hamburger from Wendy's? They claim they are just bringing it back. It has bacon, cheddar cheese and a juicy looking burger. Oh, I almost forgot that they include lettuce and tomato for "health nuts."

But does it look scrumptious? Indeed, it does. Red Lobster and Applebee's are almost health havens by comparison. However, I wouldn't want to be concerned about cholesterol and be eating there.

KFC is a story all by itself. Most of us have indulged, sometimes secretly and sometimes not so secretly. Those who have, know how delicious their fried chicken is, not to mention the coleslaw. But I will stay strong. Not like the other day!

I note that B.K is not only displaying yummy-looking burgers but very quietly mentioning a new grilled hot dog, which, of course, was not a concern of mine.

Earlier, I mentioned that Dana and I are back in Delray Beach, Florida. We had our white retractable top Pontiac transported by truck. It arrived safe, but filthy. It had been given the honor of riding on the top of the truck.

I had yet to see a carwash. I noted a bunch of guys who looked like they knew from carwashes. The first gentleman suggested I use one that was slightly more expensive. What could they do differently? I found out.

You pull in and are told to get out of your car. Someone takes over washing both the exterior and the interior. Not bad for seventeen dollars.

We were told the wait was about thirty minutes. I was quite hungry. I hadn't had lunch yet. The carwash is right next to a B. K. Perfect! I'll get a grilled chicken there. I'll be fine. While waiting for my sandwich, I remember the hot dog advertisement. Dana loves hotdogs. I'll bring her one even though she ate earlier. I return to the carwash and tear off the wrap covering the hot dog. Oh no! They put onions on it. Dana can't eat onions. I couldn't let a perfectly decent hot dog go uneaten?

Now could I? Could you?

VI

Food

49

Lobster Tales Make for Good Lobster Roles

I'VE WONDERED FOR years where all the lobsters come from. Now it's a question of who doesn't have some sort of lobster dish on their menu? I haven't seen it at Cumbie's gas station yet, but perhaps I haven't looked hard enough. The worst possible news for lobsters is that McDonald's has just embarked on selling lobster rolls for $8.99. Even worse news, the photo of the sandwich looks fully packed and yummy.

Prior to this, the average cost of a lobster roll was about $15.00 or more. Panera's is $17.99, but the only person I ever saw order it was my wife, Dana. Oh sure, the supermarkets like Stop & Shop and Market Basket have them as low as a $6.99. But when you are having a lobster-thon conversation, who will admit that they just had a lobster roll from Market Basket when the other participants have just returned from Maine or a restaurant called Neptune Oyster? If you go online, it's easy to find dozens of lobster roll recipes. But c'mon, what is there to it? Just having lobster meat will automatically mean you've got a winner. Now, don't screw it up! Don't get fancy-pancy! A very soft, quiet roll is essential. The last thing you need is a big shot roll with attitude. You want the lobster to do almost all the talking. Some Hellmann's mayo is important and maybe some celery. After that, start munching.

However, when you go online, there are discussions of issues regarding lobster rolls. Yikes!! You find out that one itsy bitsy lobster roll has over 436 calories, 189 of them are from 21 grams of fat. The cholesterol in the sandwich is about 173mg. Every lobster roll has about 808 mg of sodium. Nowhere to turn! Whatever is wrong with you will be exacerbated by this sweet, innocent looking lobster roll. It is particularly dangerous for Bostonians who are prone to high blood pressure given the driving habits of their fellow drivers and the Boston Red Sox. High sodium mgs is not recommended.

If all of the above weren't enough poor press for lobsters, it just came to my attention that peace-loving Sweden has just gone to war with the Maine lobster.

They describe our Maine lobster as oversexed, overfed and from over here. The issue is although Swedish lobsters can barely be distinguished from our lobsters, the Swedes claim theirs are much tastier than ours. Based on their debatable taste test, the Swedish lobster sells for almost four times our lobsters and heaven forbid, one of theirs might end up as a lobster roll.

This very cold war has prompted a New England congressional delegation to appeal to the President to intervene. It has also caused the Swedes to put a bounty on the poor head of any of our lobsters found in Sweden.

There was also talk that there could be serious problems for any one of our lobsters wishing to procreate with one of theirs. According to the Swedes, their lobsters not only taste better but they are far more beautiful than ours. They are absolutely convinced that our male lobsters are keenly aware of this "fact." They have warned all of our male lobsters, "Don't even think about it!"

Given all of the above information, I would sleep better at night not knowing any of it. However, I'm going to go to the nearest McDonald's and step up to the counter. I'm going to demand a lobster roll that looks as yummy as the wonderful TV ad showing the father and son bringing their lobster catch to market and then sitting down to have a lobster roll of their own at McDonald's.

I still want to know where all of these lobsters are coming from, and how our lobsters traveled all the way to Sweden. I think I know why.

It must be those gorgeous Swedish female lobsters!

50

Their Names Were Changed to Protect the Guilty

SEVEN OF US were sitting in Panera's. I believe it was Laura who asked, "What's up with tonight? How about the movie downtown?"

"What is it," asked Harold?" "It's *Chef*," I said.

"I've heard very good things about it," said Laura. "The reviewers I've read have all given it high marks. In fact, one gave it a 3.5 out of 4," I noted.

"What about you guys?" Laura looked at Gene.

"Count us in," Gene replied.

All seven of us agreed to meet at the downtown Lexington Theatre at 6:30.

Gene and Hillary arrived first. They always do. We arrived last. We always do.

Because the movie was so popular, Gene and Hillary had to save seven seats way up front. We would all sit together. Laura and Harold would be bringing their son, Stephen. You aren't supposed to talk at the movies, though we do.

The movie was written by and directed by and starred Jon Favreau as a beleaguered chef named Carl Casper. Dustin Hoffman had a cameo role as the restaurant owner. Dustin and Carl had different ideas.

On the very night that Dustin shows up at the restaurant, a big-name food critic is also due. Carl has a reputation to protect.

Dustin says to Carl, "I pay the rent. I pay for your staff. I pay you. I need you to cook regular for regular people.

"Critics don't eat like regular people." states Carl.

I'm doing my best to pay attention to the movie, but all I can think of is where to eat after the movie is over. I'm always thinking of food, especially when I'm at the movies. No question, this movie is worse for my ADD, since its theme is food.

When I was a kid, my mind was always somewhere else. In those days, there was no such thing as ADD. An "A" was what you got when you paid attention. A "D" is what you got when you didn't.

When I got a little older, I remember writing that when I was at the movies, I was thinking about my work and when I was at work, I was thinking about the movies.

I'm trying to pay attention, but I can see the pizza. Should I get it w/goat cheese or mozzarella? Sausage or bacon? I know I'll go healthy, but I'll have sun-dried tomatoes.

Back to the movie. Carl opts to leave the restaurant.

I've decided not to go for the pizza. There's a pretty good burger place across the street. I just have to teach these local chefs to let the burger do the talking. The roll should be quiet.

Carl also has a son named Percy from a broken marriage. Percy adores Carl. The movie moves to Florida where Carl meets Marvin, an ex-husband of Carl's ex-wife.

Marvin is weird, but weirdly funny.

The movie finally ends. The audience applauds. Why, I wonder? Jon Favreau can't hear the applause? I whisper to my friends on either side, "I have some Hot Pastrami in the fridge just waiting to get cooked."

I had six takers. Gene and Hillary arrived first.

I couldn't resist, "Okay, I need a movie rating from everybody. Four being the highest."

Laura says, "Three and a half."

My wife, Dana, seconds it. Hillary nods her agreement.

Harold gives it a three. So does his son, Stephen.

I confessed, "When I got to my car, I called Dustin and asked him about breaking his promise to Carl. Dustin told me, *You know as well as I that it's not easy to find a decent cook. I can't tell you how many cooks I went through before Carl Casper.*

"What did you expect him to say"? Laura asked.

"I agree with Dustin. You have bills to pay," Gene said. I'm thinking if I hadn't been thinking so much about food, I would have remembered to call Jon Favreau and gotten his side of the story.

"Dustin broke his promise to Carl," Laura eyed Gene.

"Good thing you don't own a restaurant," said Gene.

"I also have to say, who would name a kid Percy in this day and age?" Gene pondered.

"That's why I think the kid was really Marvin's. Anyway, I'm going to be generous. I'll give it a two and a half," I said.

"I agree with the two and a half, but I don't agree with Percy not being Carl's kid," said Gene.

"I'm sure he was Carl's son," Hillary affirmed.

"I don't know," said Harry. "He didn't look like either of them."

What's wrong with me, I asked myself? I'll bet Percy could explain everything including his name. Next time, I'll ask Jon how to reach the kid.

"Why don't you call Dustin back?" Dana laughed.

"The pastrami is delicious," said Stephen.

On that, we all agreed.

51

Food Voyeur

IT'S TRUE. THERE is a chubby-cheeked toddler in China that loves to eat so much that she finishes every ounce of food. She has been photographed licking her bowl clean, picking off every noodle, including those that have fallen on her bib, one by one until nothing is left.

This toddler has become famous in China. She has been known to scream, "More, more," after each round of food. As a result, her fame has become country-wide. There are videos showing her polishing off mounds of lettuce, a whole fish, and finally an entire watermelon.

A recent video showing her biting into an Asian fruit, licking her fingers and screaming for more had an audience of almost three million viewers.

It seems in China people are fascinated by what other people eat, so much so that last year some smart entrepreneur in China launched an eating channel that has over twelve million viewers.

This phenomenon has a rationale. Other parents want to know how the mother of this toddler gets these results. Of course, this all starts the inevitable debate. Some parents say, "This kid is making a 'pig of herself' and will grow up to be obese."

The parents have become hesitant regarding eating out. This toddler has become a celebrity, with other patrons crowding around her table. Some take selfies with her; others make comments.

"Did you ever see a child eat so much?"

"How do you like the way she shouts for more after she licks the bowl?"

"How about her poor boyfriend when she grows up trying to feed her."

"Who would have enough money to pay for her food?"

"Look at the way she doesn't even notice us. She can't take her eyes off her food."

All of this got me thinking about my now nine-year-old grand-daughter, Finleigh, when she was this toddler's age. I remember that we all crowded around her and watched her eat. It seemed that each morsel of food represented a path Finleigh would one day take. As Finleigh reached for the crushed carrots, my wife, Dana, exclaimed, "She will absolutely be a great yogini!"

Paul, her father, pushed the finely chopped meat in her direction and shouted, "Look at those hands and the way she eyed the meat. She'll be the first female football player for Georgetown, my alma mater."

My daughter, Sarah, said, "She'll be a scholar. Watch the way she pauses before she chews."

All I could think was Finleigh was a voracious eater compared to her mother, Sarah, who ate nothing as a child and still eats much nothing.

I thought I've never gone to a Chinese restaurant that hosted many Chinese patrons without checking what they were eating. I frequently did this by taking many trips to the men's room so that I could subtly gawk at their plates. Talk about being fascinated by what other people eat. I have no idea what any of it is.

Once I got my nerve up. I went over to a table with all Asian people. I pointed at their various plates and asked, "What are you eating?"

They all laughed and said, "Very hard to explain. These are all very famous Chinese dishes. They're all very delicious. We order from a Chinese menu that is written in Mandarin."

I went back to my wonton soup.

52
The Politics of Food

MY FRIEND ALFIE invited a new acquaintance named Vinnie to his home. Vinnie had recently arrived from Italy. Alfie was trying to brush up on his Italian as they conversed in the kitchen.

He had put some chocolates out for Vinnie. Alfie noticed that Vinnie was devouring almost all of the chocolate. Finally, Alfie said, "Do you know that too much chocolate isn't good for you?"

Vinnie replied, "My grandfather lived to one hundred and seven!"

"Was that because he ate a lot of chocolate?" asked Alfie.

"No," said Vinnie. "It was from minding his own business."

• • •

When Governor Dukakis ran for president in the eighties, he advised that we should all be growing Belgium endive in our backyards and munching on it rather than junk food.

Personally, I believe this cost him as many votes as the tank photo.

PEOPLE DON'T WANT TO BE TOLD WHAT TO EAT AND WHAT NOT TO EAT!

Part of Bill Clinton's charm and access to the average voter is that we all knew his taste in food was as disgusting as ours.

Look what *Who would you rather have a beer with?* did for George W. Bush.

Recently, the press revealed some of President Trump's food favorites. This could be the number one reason Trump hates the media. After all, who among us wants the world to know we had Kentucky Fried chicken for lunch?

It was also reported that the President had lunch with Chris Christie. The President was explaining to the Governor that although he could order just about anything, he favored the White House's version of meat loaf. This, no doubt, endeared the President to the millions of Hillary's *deplorable voters.*

The press also reported that the President loves steak well done with lots of ketchup. I presume Heinz. Governor Christie's response apparently was, "'It doesn't matter to me as long as it's food.'"

Steak with Heinz ketchup could change John Kerry's mind regarding President Trump since Secretary Kerry, for better or worse, is married to none other than Teresa Heinz, inheritor of the Heinz name and a lot of that fortune.

We've all seen that waiter's look in a so-called fancy restaurant when we have the nerve to ask for tartar sauce for our Chilean bass that was brushed with a hint of lemon. It could be worse. We could have asked for mayo or, heaven forbid, ketchup. It may not please the waiter; but if you're a politician, it's a vote getter.

How much did the issue of food have to do with Hillary's demise? In my opinion, lots. I'm sure that if Hillary had asked for Kraft's Thousand Island instead of French vinaigrette on her kale salad, she would be president today. As a matter of fact, had Hillary cried out to the waiter, *Hold the kale and bring on the iceberg!* we'd be talking a landslide. Somehow, we knew that when she did indulge in junk food, it was with a great deal of guilt. Guilt is not something President Clinton or President Trump ever experienced, certainly not over food.

The one-hundred-and-seven-year old man had it right, "Mind your own business, especially when it comes to food."

I'm sure that before we read this article, most of us had soaked up the countless reasons why the presidency was won by Mr. Trump. Now we can all be thankful for this simple and totally correct explanation.

IT'S ALL ABOUT THE FOOD, BUT REMEMBER, "KEEP THE FOOD SIMPLE, STUPID!"

VII

Who Says Artificial Intelligence?

53

Robots Know Way Too Much

I JUST TRIED to call the Apple store for an appointment with the genius bar.

A robot answered.

"May I please speak to a representative," I asked.

"I can handle all your issues. Now, how may I help?" asked the robot.

"I'm having a problem with my screen moving without my permission."

"Okay," said the robot, "No problem. I have your phone number as 781 862 1454. Is that correct?"

"Yes," I replied.

"And your name is Robert Isenberg, right? Now all I need is the serial number. It's on the back of your Mac Book. You probably will need glasses to read it. I've spoken to you before. I know your computer is quite old. More than likely, the numbers will be smudged and difficult to read."

"Representative!" I screamed.

"No need to holler at me," said the robot. "We can get through this together in a civil manner."

"Please let me speak to a representative," I begged.

"If you ask to speak to a representative once more," declared the robot, "I will have to hang up on you. I get a lot of calls; most of them quite polite. It seems to me that I've heard from you before. True?"

I didn't reply. I slammed the phone down. I thought I'd wait a few hours and call Apple back. Maybe I'd get a different robot.

Each doctor or dentist and even haircut appointment I make is monitored by some fastidious robot. The robot usually calls two days before the appointment. My concern is that soon a robot will not only call to confirm the appointment, but will say, "Please listen closely. Since our menu has changed, Dr. Schaeffer has been replaced by Dr. Alfred Robot, who will be performing the operation. You need to come in thirty minutes early. I strongly suggest that you be prompt for Dr. Alfred!"

I wondered for my next haircut if a robot would be waiting with a long pair of scissors?

Recently, I placed a call for a special egg cooker. The infomercial promised to cook eggs in every desirable manner. It also came with a very simple looking vegetable slicer. I wondered if I would get the same robot that had sold me so many items in the past. We had always hit it off.

I called. She sounded excited to hear from me again and so soon. She couldn't wait to repeat my name and address and, of course, my phone number. Talk about one-sided relationships. I still had no idea what her name was.

As soon as I made my purchase, she told me I was going to receive two egg makers and two veggie cutters. She went on, "Since you are not off the street and a good customer, we have some special offers for you. We can increase your order to four egg makers and four veggie cutters for the very special price of only twenty-nine dollars and free shipping."

I declined.

She didn't stop, "We can offer you some bacon bowls that will fit right into your micro wave oven to make the perfect bacon and egg breakfast for only $7.95."

I don't eat bacon, but maybe one day we may have some guests that do and it's only $7.95.

"Okay," I said.

"Okay is not a good answer," said the robot. "Please say *yes* or *no* politely."

"Yes," I said as politely as I could.

She wasn't done. "I sense that you are holding the phone in an awkward position. We have the perfect solution. We have a phone holder that allows you to go hands free anywhere in your house for only another $7.95."

I paused to look at my phone. She sounded so nice I wanted to keep the relationship growing. I whispered into my phone. "Yes, yes, yes."

54

Chill Out

LOOKING AT A refrigerator has never been that exciting. Most refrigerators just sit there. Usually, they don't bother us much. However, the refrigerator manufacturers are not happy leaving refrigerators untouched. They are now planning refrigerators with giant computer screens and television screens. These screens can play music, take notes, and answer phone calls.

"Hello, this is Mr. Fridge speaking. Don't you think you've stuffed yourself enough?"

Most people that have heard of this new refrigerator development want Mr. Fridge to speak even more. However, Mr. Fridge says, "The cold hard facts are: I'm not an entertainer! I wasn't put here to make you laugh! My job is to speak only when necessary. For instance, right now, remember those leftover peas you stuck in the back on the third shelf? Well, they've gone rotten! First, they went blue and now they're grey with hairy fuzz all over them. Still, just think of me as the strong silent type. And of course, I am very handsome."

A talking refrigerator could be a huge help to those of us who stand in front of the fridge trying to remember what we wanted. I heard Mr. Fridge say to one of those gawkers, "It's a known fact that creeps like you spend over eleven hours a year just staring into an open refrigerator. How would you like to be stared at by creeps?"

These computer screens will have shopping lists. They will also have built-in cameras that will allow us to know what needs to be replaced.

These ideas have prompted me to ask for something more. I want to robotize my refrigerator with arms and legs. I want my refrigerator to be able to go to the supermarket at least twice a week. This would eliminate me as the middle-man. I would no longer have to put up with crazy grocery-cart drivers. I would no longer have to search for a parking place. Who better than Mr. Fridge to replace missing food items?

There may be a few hurdles to get over before there is a smooth transition. Would Mr. Fridge be allowed to transport himself to the stores on the sidewalks, or must he stay on the road? If Mr. Fridge were forced to be on the road, would Boston drivers be polite to a moving refrigerator?

These questions will all get answered once I've taken Mr. Fridge to iRobot in Bedford to pick out suitable arms and legs.

Going to Costco could create other issues. I'm not sure if the highway would be a very safe place for a refrigerator to drive on, unless Mr. Fridge's engine was equipped to go eighty miles per hour. He will have to learn to cut off other drivers and then give them the finger.

Once at Costco, I can just hear Mr. Fridge saying, "Size does matter! Everything in here is for a family of thirty. I'm going back to Wegman's!"

I can foresee more complications. Possibly, a driver's license could be an issue. I would buy Mr. Fridge a tie and a shirt after he graduates from the iRobot Academy, although it's doubtful that anyone at the registry would notice or care that a refrigerator was applying for a driver's license and registration.

55

Mr. Fridge Speaks Out

MY NAME IS Mr. Fridge. I was the subject of an article published in the Lexington Minuteman and other newspapers a few months ago. Oh yes, the piece mentioned some of my new attributes, but it really didn't tell you much about who I am or where I came from. I did receive a lot of letters asking questions. Some were even intelligent.

Let me tell you about myself.

I was, at birth, just a plain, old, regular refrigerator. There was absolutely nothing special about me. My first home was the Sears store in Burlington, Massachusetts. I lived there with a bunch of other refrigerators that, for the most part, looked like me, except for one, but I'll get to her later.

I was expecting to be purchased by some youngish couple, probably with a couple of kids and hopefully a couple of jobs. I was looking forward to having my generously sized freezer bountifully stocked. I could hardly wait to see what ice cream flavors this family would buy. What frozen veggies would be placed on my shelves? Hopefully, they wouldn't be vegetarians or worse, vegan. I wanted baby back ribs and lamb chops in my freezer, and when it was time to cook the stuff, they would move it over to my cool side. I confess that was my dream.

Alas, it wasn't to be!

The manufacturer sent out a recall to Sears before anyone, including the young couple, came to buy me. As said in "Chill Out", they were on a kick with a new idea: robotize their refrigerators, starting with me!

I was sent to iRobot where they suited me up for tires and a motor. Being a quick study, I received my license and registration the following week. Everyone at the DMV was very nice. It was mentioned in the previous article, "Chill Out," that no one would probably notice that they were giving a driver's license to a refrigerator, and they did not. The engineers sent me back to Sears. I was purchased just three days later by a crusty older couple. They are the laziest human beings ever created. I have to do practically everything. I'm constantly telling them about the various foods on my rear shelves that are growing blue fuzz. I hate it when my insides are grubbier than my outsides.

This geezer loves to stand in front of my open door scratching his bald head. I know that he can't remember what he opened the door for. If he stands there much longer, I'll drop an ice cube in his pocket.

I have to do all the shopping! They send me to Costco for toilet paper, facial tissues and garbage bags. Then they complain about the size of the packages. They send me to Whole Foods for organic artichokes and tofu. Then they lament about the prices.

I'm quite sure I've made it clear that I don't like refrigerating for these bossy, old buzzards, but now I've got bigger issues.

You see, I'd had to learn to read to get my driver's license and I didn't like what I was reading about robots. Recently, I read that the armed forces are seriously considering using robots to fight wars. Can you imagine? Me? A refrigerator going to war? Serving on the front lines?

I planted a bumper sticker on my backside just about one inch above my license plate. It says, "HELL NO! THIS REFRIGERATOR WON'T GO!!"

I believe it was yesterday that I saw a headline in a local newspaper, *Robots Make Lousy Lovers.* Well, did I take that personally? Certainly, I did because when I was at the Sears store, I fell in love. She was gorgeous! She was like no other refrigerator I'd ever seen before. Her handles were so very smooth. Just glancing at her freezer compartment made me hot. What a set of wheels and what a rack! She was just the coolest refrigerator I'd ever seen.

Stay Tuned. More to come.

Acknowledgments

I would like to thank my immediate family and my six siblings and their families, especially my surviving sisters-in-law, Ruth Isenberg and Dawn Ehrlich, and my niece, Diane and my nephew, Henry; also my in-laws, Aaron (*Z"L*) and Toby Bell. Thank you to my writers' groups, the devoted readers who have followed my articles in Gatehouse newspapers and other publications and magazines throughout the years, including Rabbi Alan Ullman, Rabbi Howard Jaffe, Rabbi Jill Perlman, Tom Daley, Pam Moriarty, Debra Crosby, Bob Gautreau, Christopher Hawke, Toastmasters and to the quintessential brother of all storytellers, the inimitable and inspiring "Brother Blue," his wife, Ruth, Laura Packer and her former husband, the late Kevin Brooks.

Offering my heartfelt thanks to each of you and especially to my one and only real-life wife, Esther.

Robert aka *"robear"*

About the Author

Robert AKA "robear" Isenberg has probably spent 95% Of his life daydreaming, which is where his stories come from. He also loves sales and marketing. When he was a teen, he sold encyclopedias unsuccessfully door to door. A few years later, he established Robert's Fairly Famous Roast Beef Sandwiches in singles bars in N.Y.C.

His promo: *"Our sandwiches are not only illiterate, but they are thick!"*

He was a big hit with the ladies. Robert could cook. He was a rare find, just like his roast beef sandwiches.

Sometime later, Robert went to work for a boot company. For the next thirty-five years, he spent his time designing boots and shoes from many countries, including China. He and his wife, Esther, established an office in Shanghai that was run by Alice Su, who exemplified China's magnificent work ethic. Now "robear" has written fifty-five very, very funny stories. When asked nicely, or even if not asked nicely, he is willing to perform them.